ABOUT NABAT BOOKS

NABAT BOOKS is a series dedicated to reprinting forgotten memoirs by various misfits, outsiders, and rebels. The underlying concept is based on a few simple propositions:

That to be a success under the current definition is highly toxic – wealth, fame and power are a poison cocktail; that this era of triumphal capitalism glorifies the most dreary human traits like greed and self-interest as good and natural; that the "winners" version of reality and history is deeply lame and soul-rotting stuff. Given this, it follows that the truly interesting and meaningful lives and real adventures are only to be had on the margins of what Kenneth Rexroth called "the social lie". It's with the dropouts, misfits, dissidents, renegades and revolutionaries, against the grain, between the cracks and amongst the enemies of the state that the good stuff can be found. Fortunately there is a mighty subterranean river of testimony from the disaffected, a large cache of hidden history, of public secrets overlooked by the drab conventional wisdom that Nabat books aims to tap into. A little something to set against the crushed hopes, mountains of corpses, and commodification of everything. Actually, we think, it's the best thing western civilization has going for itself.

T0272825

Beggars of Life
A Hobo Autobiography

Other Books in the Nabat Series

BEGGARS OF LIFE
A HOBO AUTOBIOGRAPHY

JIM TULLY

INTRODUCTION BY CHARLES WILLEFORD

AK PRESS / NABAT

EDINBURGH, LONDON, AND OAKLAND

2004

This edition copyright © 2004 Nabat/AK Press
1st Nabat Edition

First published 1924 by Albert & Charles Boni
Holistic Barbarian Reprinted by permission of JET Literary
Associates, Inc.

Beggars of Life

ISBN 1 902593 78 2

AK Press   AK Press
674 A 23rd Street   PO Box 12766
Oakland CA   Edinburgh, Scotland
94612-1163 USA   EH8 9YE

A catalogue record for this title is available from the
Library of Congress
Library of Congress Control Number: 2003112985

Series editor: Bruno Ruhland
Cover, cover art, book, and series design donated by
fran sendbuehler, mouton-noir – montréal

If you know of any memoirs by misfits, outsiders, or subversive
types that deserve to be back in print, please write to Bruno at
AK Press in Oakland.

Prisoners can receive this book by sending $10.00 to
AK Press at the Oakland address noted above.

To Rupert Hughes
A Friend
And
Charlie Chaplin
A Mighty Vagabond

TRAVEL

The railroad track is miles away,
And the day is loud with voices speaking,
Yet there isn't a train goes by all day
But I hear its whistle shrieking.
All night there isn't a train goes by,
Though the night is still for sleep and dreaming,
But I see its cinders red on the sky,
And hear its engine steaming.
My heart is warm with the friends I make,
And better friends I'll not be knowing,
Yet there isn't a train I wouldn't take,
No matter where it's going

Edna St. Vincent Millay

TABLE OF CONTENTS

JIM TULLY: HOLISTIC BARBARIAN
CHARLES WILLEFORD

JIM TULLY was a short stocky man, without much neck. His arms and shoulders were powerful, and he was physically strong from driving tent stakes, making chains, fighting, and hanging on to the iron ladders of fast intercontinental freights. His kinky red hair, too thick to be combed, resembled Elsa Lanchester's electrified hair in the movie *Bride of Frankenstein*.

A cheerful, cynical stoic, he believed in nothing – or so he claimed – and in no one other than himself. Like Jack London, Jack Black, and Josiah Flynt, Tully was a road kid who found a way to get off the road. He learned how to write.

In 1943, Damon Runyon, in a burst of enthusiasm, placed Jim Tully among the top five American writers.

H. L. Mencken, who was one of the first of many editors to recognize Jim Tully's ability, published Tully in the closing issue of *Smart Set,* and featured many of the vagabond tales during his long editorship of *The American Mercury.* Mencken wrote, "If Jim Tully were a Russian, read in translation, all the professors would be hymning him. He has all of Gorky's capacity for making vivid the miseries of poor and helpless men, and in addition he has a humor that no Russian could conceivably have."

Louis Kronenberger described Tully's writing as "a succession of direct hard blows from the shoulder. The prose has the defiant blare of trumpets; all of it is speed and force and action. It is not art. But it is the creative and compelling journalism of a creative mind."

For every booster, Tully had a half-dozen detractors, and many critics despised him for his arrogance. To the general reading public, Tully was a curiosity, a tramp who wrote about a lifestyle they hadn't known about. They bought his books eagerly. Tully's uncommon adjustment to his rapidly changing times, together with his disinterested observation of life, indicate a much finer intelligence than he was ever given credit for during his lifetime.

Jim Tully was born near St. Mary's, Ohio, June 3, ca. 1891. As a result of a lingering heart ailment, he died June 22, 1947, in Hollywood. His death made headlines in many metropolitan newspapers, and a fair evaluation of his life and work was printed in the *New York Times*. Today his name is forgotten by contemporary readers, and all of his books are out of print.

But the critical neglect of this important American writer is understandable. Tully was a paradox. Together with Dashiell Hammett, Tully was one of the founders of the hard-boiled school of writers in the U.S., but his earlier important work has been overshadowed by the personality features he wrote for national magazines during his later years in Hollywood. During twenty-one years as a full-time professional writer, Tully made two fortunes: one as a leader in the field of naturalist – "proletarian" – fiction and non-fiction, and the second by describing the shallow lives of Hollywood movie stars and other celebrities for mass circulation magazines.

Although his personality feature articles postdate his superior autobiographical books, he commanded top prices in both writing fields. Tully evaluated people as he saw them, not as they saw themselves, and, in America, "new" journalism was a highly original approach to non-fiction. How he felt personally about the people he interviewed frequently made him unfair to his subjects. For example, he downgraded Arnold Bennett when he interviewed him in London, because the novelist had none of Tully's books on his shelves. Tully was both feared and hated as an interviewer, but he was never turned down because it was prestigious to have an article by Tully published in a national magazine.

As an Irishman, Tully had little compunction about making a good story better than it already was by exaggerating the facts, but he had very little imagination. One critic called him a "frustrated novelist," a comment the author resented bitterly. But the observation was fair. Tully's mind was too literal for imaginative, inventive fiction. The vivid characterization of the movie director in his novel *Jarnegan* was practically a step-by-step biography of Jim *(The Covered Wagon)* Cruze. To provide the gauche director with needed touches of sensitivity, Tully snatched tracer elements from the life of his friend, Paul Bern (Irving Thalberg's right-hand man and "artistic conscience.")

Tully's first novel, *Emmett Lawler,* was a barely disguised autobiographical account of his dreary boyhood in an orphan home, of slave labor on the isolated farm of a maniac, followed by sketchy incidents of his later life as road kid, factory slave, tramp, circus roustabout, and professional fighter. He knew so little about writing at the time, the first draft of *Emmett Lawler* was one 100,000 word paragraph. *Emmett Lawler,* however, adumbrates his later autobiographical books, and its publication in 1922 was the beginning of his writing career.

As he matured and developed his spare, blunt style, Tully returned to his vagabond years for the material of his best autobiographical books – *Beggars of Life, Shanty Irish, Circus Parade, Shadows of Men,* and *Blood on the Moon.* Altogether, counting Broadway plays and other works he wrote in collaboration with Robert Nichols, Frank Dazey, and Charles Behan, twenty-nine books were published under Tully's name. In his best books, Tully had the ability to uproot the reader from a comfortable environment, to make him feel and live with his men of the road, the jail, and the professional boxing ring.

The son of a ditch-digger, and the grandson of another, Tully was never impressed by the near great nor even by the truly great. From boyhood he called himself "Jim." When a New York critic asked him why he didn't use his full name on his books, he said, "They call servants 'James.'"

Writing was hard for Tully, and he often worked sixteen hours a day at his desk, writing and revising his work. As a consequence, his work holds up very well today, including his ephemeral magazine articles – and he was published in more than forty magazines.

Yesterday I reread "An Ex-Hobo Looks at America" (*Scribner's,* Sept., 1927). I was surprised at his insights, and by how little social conditions have changed in America since 1927. Our political-industrial-military-academic complex is virtually the same. Wealthy men are still given probation, and poor men still go to prison; working men are still exploited , and only second-rate men with second-rate minds enter politics.

Every year I receive from thirty to fifty "examination" copies of new college readers. It is hard to tell one reader from another. The articles and essays are the same ("Shooting an Elephant"), the stories are the same ("The Killers"), and the poems are the same ("The Red Wheelbarrow"). It would be a pleasant relief to see "An Ex-Hobo Looks at America" reprinted in one of these college readers, even if it did disturb Business Administration majors.

Tully rarely worked at a regular job before he became a writer, nor did he consider himself a migratory worker (hobo). He was a road kid, and then a tramp – a beggar. But because the general public does not make the distinction between "hobo" and "bum," he was never able to escape the appellation of "hobo," a term his publishers considered more colorful. This distinction was important to Tully. A hobo is primarily a worker, a field hand who rides freight trains from one poorly paying job to another to save money. In time, or if he was fortunate, the hobo obtained a permanent job and never rode freights again. In other words, the hobo was – and is – an establishment hopeful looking for an establishment. A road kid and a tramp are professional bums who have chosen the road as a way of life, or, more often than not, it has chosen them. The tramp, or professional bum, is proud – as Tully was proud – of his rejection of society, and of society's rejection of him. But it is a hard way to live; only a bitter man can stay on the road for a lifetime.

During Tully's many years on the bum he spent most of his idle time in public libraries. And, when he left a library, he usually took a couple of books with him – hidden under his jacket. He once stole a two-volume, illustrated edition of *Paradise Lost.* He needed enough reading material to last him for a long freight train trip to the coast. The would-be writer invariably does a lot of indiscriminate reading before he tries to write anything himself, and Tully had always wanted to be a writer, a notion he got from the success of Jack London.

Road kids, professional criminals, dope addicts, radio announcers, writers, and other society misfits who are constitutionally unable or unwilling to hold a regular job, spend many fruitful hours in public libraries. Self-educated writers like Jim Tully get strange educations through voluminous, undirected reading. No other American writer had as little formal preparation for writing; but he had persuaded himself that he could become a writer. His wide range of reading gave him a veneer of culture that astonished the society and literary figures he met after his initial successes. Frank Scully, Damon Runyon, and particularly Arnold Bennett, were charmed by Tully's self-confidence, social ease, and wide range of knowledge. The only man he never impressed was his good friend Wilson Mizener, who accused Tully of not having a bath until he was thirty, and called him a "porter in the bawdy house of words."

Tully held a variety of menial, nondescript jobs, but finally learned how to make chains in Ohio. Although he never became an expert at this trade, he confessed to Sara Haardt, he learned it well enough to dodge the draft during World War I by becoming a government chain inspector – a "war-essential" draft-exempt position. It is interesting to note that he kept his union card and dues as a chain-maker up-to-date at the height of his career, when he was averaging $80,000 a year from his writing. Making chains is highly skilled work, and expert chain-makers were proud of their prowess at this difficult craft. Tully describes these craftsmen at some length in *Blood on the Moon,* and he was rightfully proud of his union card. But a permanent job as a chain-maker was unsuitable for a man of his temperament.

After more than seven straight years on the road, including a stint as a circus roustabout and stake driver, Tully tried another path to success that is always open to the poor and uneducated in America – the professional prize ring. Gentle Joe Gans had given him a few professional tips on boxing in Chicago, and Tully had served a willing apprenticeship in street fights and rough-and-tumbles. He knew that he could hit hard and absorb punishment, and those are adequate qualifications for any would-be club fighter. In a newspaper print shop, Tully faked some newsclippings that "proved" a record of thirty winning fights without a single loss. Armed with these phony clippings, he began to fight professionally, as a featherweight, in Cleveland. Some twenty fights later, after fighting under an assumed name in San Francisco, he regained consciousness in his hotel room. He had been unconscious for almost twenty-four hours. His watch and the purse he had received for the fight had been stolen from him. He quit the ring forever, determined to become a writer.

Ten years later his first book was published.

While he learned his craft, he became an itinerant tree surgeon. This is seasonal work, for the most part, and between jobs Tully worked on his first book until it was finished. Realizing that he needed editorial help, he went first to Harold Bell Wright, in Los Angeles, and then to Upton Sinclair. Wright advised him not to write in the first person, and Sinclair refused to read the manuscript. Finally, Rupert Hughes, the "reactionary," helped him by going over the 100,000 words with a blue pencil, gave him money when he was destitute, and stuck with him faithfully through the difficult revisions of *Emmett Lawler.*

Tully's first publisher didn't give him an advance, and even after the book came out he was still broke in Hollywood. Ralph Block, who had faith in Tully's ability, introduced him to Charlie Chaplin. Chaplin, then at the height of his fame, hired Tully as his press agent at fifty dollars a week. Chaplin, whose background of poverty was similar to Tully's, liked to have

Tully in his entourage, although he didn't care for his writing. During the eighteen months Tully was employed to write articles for Chaplin's signature, the comedian signed only one of them.

Once, when Tully slept soundly throughout a story conference on The Gold Rush, Chaplin said, "You're a snob, Jim." A few years later, when Tully wrote Chaplin's biography, he admitted that this was the only compliment Chaplin had ever given him.

Chaplin was angered enough by Tully's unauthorized version of his life to sue the writer for a half-million dollars. Chaplin lost the suit. The biography was true, if unflattering, and Tully's Chaplin biography is a must book for our burgeoning crop of cinema historians.

Like many self-educated writers, Tully was chary of English grammar and syntax, and avoided compound sentences. His paragraphs were rarely more than three sentences in length, a practice he learned from writing newspaper publicity releASES. OFTEN EACH SENTENCE WAS ITS OWN PARAGRAPH, CONTAINING A SINGLE THOUGHT. DESPITE HIS LARGE READING VOCABULARY, TULLY WROTE AS IF HE WERE RESTRICTED TO THE BASIC ENGLISH LIST OF 850 WORDS.

HE WAS ALSO FOND OF THE OROTUND CLICHÉ, AND HE INVENTED MANY OF THEM. HIS PROSE IS FILLED WITH TERSE, ONE-LINE PARAGRAPHS. HE USED THESE SHORT LINES TO DRIVE HOME POINTS THAT HAD ALREADY BEEN MADE. WHEN THEY WORK THEY ARE POWERFUL.

"HE IS IMPERSONAL AS WEATHER."

"Winchell, for once, was silent."

"He did not move or speak again."

Even out of context these are strong sentences. The cumulative effect of these short sentences in a full-length book is sometimes overwhelming. There are powerful, single chapters in all of his books, but many chapters are uneven in a full-length book, and some chapters are ragged.

Unimaginative, wit did not come easily to Tully, although some of his epigrams are still in circulation: "Fame is merely the prolonging of neighborhood gossip."

Some of Tully's similes would make Fannie Hurst wince: "–as somnolent as an Indian," "–as still as a rural gravestone," but many of them worked. The bad ones stand out because he used so many similes.

He had the great artist's ability to capture, with a few efficient words, the essence of a man's appearance and personality. And once a reader is caught up in the story Tully tells, plangent discords are rarely bothersome. The rhythm of his writing has a poetic quality.

Tully's decline in popularity can be explained as easily as his success: He was a writer attuned to the exact instant of his times, in accord with the twenty-year cultural lag in American literature. He became popular in the mid-Twenties, and his books were popular throughout the Thirties. But the best years he wrote about were those from 1896 to 1912. His books were direct outgrowths of the pre-WW1 social system, the product of the material conditions of his youth. By the time his books appeared they were "historical" novels, but the reading public of the late Twenties and Thirties accepted them as current fare. Today they are truly historical, but they are still fresh and vital as American literary history.

Dreiser's Clyde Griffiths, Hemingway's Nick Adams, and Tully's Emmett Lawler: these are the three young literary heroes who became the prototypes for the American initiation novel of the 1896–1912 period. Clyde Griffiths, the pragmatist-sneak, and Nick Adams, the romantic, upper-middle-class rebel, are still an important duo in American literature. Their adventures are still recommended highly to college students today. But Emmett Lawler, the orphan-road kid, has been lost somewhere along the way.

I am not concerned with the adventures, or incidents, in Tully's autobiographical books – although they are of interest in themselves, from an historical point of view – my primary concern is with the attitude, the amused stoicism of the narrative "I" in his books.

We can easily understand a Nick Adams volunteering his services for a foreign army (as an ambulance driver with "officer" status, naturally, but not as a combat soldier, because that was the thing to do: See Dos Passos, e. e. cummings, etc.); and we can understand, with sympathy if not empathy, the ambition of young Clyde, who was willing to kill for plenty of dough and a neat social life. But if we don't understand Jim Tully, and the conditions that produced men like him, conditions that are producing more just like him every day – but without, as yet, his drive – we will fail to understand how at least one third of our nation feels and thinks about the American Way of Life.

It took a lot of guts to dodge the draft during World War II (remember Pearl Harbor?), but can you imagine what kind of guts it took to dodge the draft in World War I? Well, then, if you are a middle-class reader, as most readers are, ponder the indifference to public opinion of Jim Tully, examining chains during World War I, and that of his buddy, and fellow road kid, Jack Dempsey, working in the shipyards during the war that was supposed to end all wars.

Tully did not indulge in the psychographic or social overtones so popular in the fiction of the Twenties, nor did he make value judgments about yeggs, heisters, wolves, bums, club fighters, and sneak thieves in his books. By straightforward narration of the social events he knew intimately, and from firsthand experience, he made the readers of his time conscious of the social evils.

Tully's impersonal article, for example, on the legal execution by hanging of a young man in California, is as great an indictment against capital punishment as anything ever written on the subject by Albert Camus ("California Holiday," The American Mercury, Jan. 1928).

Walt Whitman said, "Literature is big only in one way – when used as an aid in the growth of the humanities – a furthering of the cause of the masses – a means whereby men may be revealed to each other as brothers."

At least five of Tully's books (*Beggars of Life, The Circus Parade, Shanty Irish, Shadows of Men, Blood on the Moon*) are within Whitman's concept of literature. These are the five books Tully wanted to have published some day as his "Underworld Edition." He thought, and in this I agree with him, that his literary reputation would rest on these five books. Today, however, as I mentioned earlier, all of Tully's books are out of print. The copyrights have expired, and his work is now up for grabs for any U. S. publisher, with a penchant for social history, to reissue.

What Jim Tully had to say about growing up absurdly in an earlier America should not be lost on today's readers. The "Underworld Edition" should be reprinted and reissued in a single inexpensive volume. For a writer of mean books, Jim Tully's achievement was not mean, but it will be demeaning to all of us if we fail to give him a second trial.

CHAPTER I
ST. MARYS

ACROSS A CHASM OF YEARS the outlines of even the most vivid life are blurred. But impressions gained as a youthful hobo are likely to endure until the rover has wandered the last road home. I have often wished that Cervantes had written a tale of his wanderings on the sunlit roads of Spain, or that Goldsmith had written in matchless English of the days when he played a flute for bread, or that blind old Homer had left a few pages about his experiences while tramping the roads of Greece. The old minstrel might even have immortalized a Greek slave who fed him.

I made three unsuccessful journeys before I finally became even an amateur hobo. For it may be recorded here that hoboes regard their chosen profession seriously. There is much to learn in the game and more to endure.

During idle hours, I loitered near the railroad yards of an Ohio town from which I launched upon my tramping career. I met hoboes there, who nonchalantly told me strange tales of far places. One youthful vagrant had tramped all the way from California. He had served two months in a western jail for vagrancy. He was proud of his exploits, and told of them grandly. He made me ashamed of a humdrum life in a humdrum town.

We sat near a high trestle which spanned the St. Marys river. The boy threw stones into the lazy water below. I watched him closely. He was rough in speech and action, as a lad might well be who had tramped from California. One of his eyes had been knocked out while he was tramping in Arkansas. He wore a leather patch over the empty red socket. It was fastened by a shoe string that was tied at the back of his head. He was a brawny youth, and sunburned. The fingers of his right hand were yellow from holding many cigarettes. He was flippant in manner, and spoke of far countries with careless gesture instead of reverence.

He sailed a flat rock into the river. It skimmed along the water like a flying fish, and at last sank in a whirling ripple.

"What burg is this, 'Bo?" he asked.

"It's St. Marys, sir," I humbly replied.

"Don't Sir me. Billy's my name," he blurted. He looked toward the town and sneered, then snorted, "Hell, I wouldn't be found dead in a joint like this. It ain't a town; it's a disease. A guy's only in the world once. He may as well lamp it over while he's at it, even if he has only got one lamp."

"Do you like it on the road, Bill?" I asked.

The boy turned his head slightly so as to get a square look at me with his one eye. "Sure I likes it. I wouldn't give it up for nothin'. They ain't nothin' in workin'. Only boobs work. Them old whistles blow ev'ry mornin' – an' they piles out like a lotta cattle. Not for Yours Truly."

"I'd like to leave this burg," I told him, "an' think I will. I darn near have to pay the factory to work there." I explained my work and wages to the boy, who smiled at me disdainfully when I had finished.

"Chuck it, Kid, chuck it. Gosh, you can't do no worse. All you're doin' here's eatin'. You kin git that anywhere. A stray cat gits that. Besides," and the boy's voice rose higher, "you're learnin' somethin' on the road. What the devil kin you learn here? I'll bet the mayor o' this burg don't know what it's all about."

I pondered over this terrible philosophy for a moment as the boy lifted the black patch and scratched the red lid of his vacant socket. There was a long silence; I resolved to leave the town as soon as I could. But the resolution was not made without some qualms. For all the nondescript people in St. Marys were my friends.

One old drunkard had drifted there, from where, no one knew. He often talked to me about books. When drunk, which was nearly every day, he bragged of his past, a tortuous, winding road, full of many a weary bog. His name was Jack Raley.

The natives of the town would tease old Raley while they bought him liquor. Though a poverty-stricken drunkard, a cadger of drinks, a cleaner of cuspidors, a mopper of bar-room floors, he was still the wealthiest man I knew in that town; – for he carried a tattered volume of Voltaire in his pocket, and he talked to me about it. Raley had been a tramp printer for years until he came to the end of the trail at St. Marys.

While the one-eyed youth remained silent, I thought of the old man who wore a thin valise strap as a belt around his torn corduroy trousers. All his front teeth were gone but two. He could easily have dispensed with them, as he seldom ate. He was a magnificent drunk-ard, quite the greatest I have ever known. His eyes were yellow, and bloodshot, and many streaks of blood ran through them like tiny red rivers through yellow fields.

Finally I said, "I'll beat it out of here all right, but I hate to leave some of the people."

Bill was aroused by the words. "Well, you can't take 'em wit' you. Forgit all that stuff. It's bunkerino."

"Yes, I guess you're right," I replied weakly.

Bill looked flabbergasted, as though amazed at the idea that any unwandered youth in a small town would question words of his. There was a challenge in his voice as he spoke, "Guess I'm right! I'll say I'm right. Huh! I know a few things. I wasn't born on Monday."

I placated him by asking questions about hobo life. The ego of the youth rose to the occasion. He told me many things, the truth of which later experiences verified.

"If you ever go on the road, Kid, don't you never let no old tramp play you for a sucker. You know, them old birds're too lazy to scratch themselves when they're crummy. So they gits young kids and teaches 'em to beg. They know people'll feed kids quicker'n they will them, so they make the kids do all the beggin'. Lotsa people pity kids at back doors. The old tramps calls the kids their punks. There's a lot of punkgrafters on the road. Lotsa things I could tell you," said the one-eyed youthful rover.

The whistle of an engine was heard in the west. Then the noise of rolling cars rumbled through the air. It vibrated along the rails of the trestle.

I watched the big engine come steaming down the tracks, with its red cars rolling behind it. A brakeman sat on top of a box car behind the engine. He held a stick in his hand, and gazed across the land-scape. I envied him.

The youth pulled the leather patch more snugly over his eye, and throwing back his shoulders, he ran with the train. Shouting, "S'long, Kid. Be good," he boarded it with a marvellous swagger, waving a cig-arette-stained hand at me as the train rolled across the trestle toward Lima.

Chapter II
Initiation

A FEW WEEKS LATER, I journeyed by freight to Muncie, Indiana, nearly seventy miles away. I paid my fare, if not to the company, at least to the train crew, by helping unload freight at each station.

All day I unloaded freight at every station at which the train stopped. It was one of those days so common in late winter throughout the Middle West. The atmosphere was murky green and neither cold nor warm. The animals huddled together in the fields, as though reluctant to break the warmth-giving habits of winter. Once I saw a feather-tossed robin perched on a wire fence along the tracks. By an odd quirk of memory I can see it to this day – it looked hopeless and woebegone – a strayed reveller who had left a warm climate too soon. The smoke from the engine rolled over it, but it did not move, and I remember thinking that perhaps the smoke made it warm.

I stood for long moments at the box-car door and gazed at the passing landscape. What did it matter though I lifted heavy boxes at every station – I was going somewhere. Over in the next valley were life and dreams and hopes. Monotony and the wretched routine of a drab Ohio town would be unknown. I, a throwback to the ancient Irish tellers of fairy tales, was at last on the way to high adventure. Sad and miserable men, broken on the wheel of labor, tired nerve-torn women too weary to look at the stars – these would not be inhabitants of the dream country to which I was going. What a picture I must have made – a heavy-jowled red-headed youth with a crooked smile and a freckled face, and clad in the cast-off clothing of more fortunate working boys. Everything seemed to pass through my mind – I was not a beggar at the gates of life – I would return to St. Marys a rich man. I would show the aristocratic girls who snubbed me on Spring Street that I was not what they thought I was, I would not come back until everybody had heard of me – and when I did come back and walked along the streets people would say – "There goes Jimmy Tully, he used to be a little drunkard and hang around Rabbit Town with the whores, and look at him now – huh – that shows what a fellow can do in this country if he works hard and saves his money." Even then, dreaming of some day being a writer, I would write great stories and my name would be in all the magazines. Some day the natives in St. Marys would wake up and see my name spread across the front page of the *Saturday Evening Post;* by God, I'd show them, I would. As the train gathered speed my thoughts came more swiftly.

I thought of Edna – Edna was, in my opinion, the prettiest little girl that ever sold her body in Rabbit Town. She used to charge the men a dollar each, and she once told me she had made forty-eight dollars one night. I glowed with satisfaction at the memory of Edna. I had first learned about sex from her. She never charged me anything. She told me that women liked red-headed guys. I saw her white body and the yellow corn-silk coloured hair falling over her shoulders and my own body thrilled with desire. Plainly it was no place to think about women – but I thought not of that. I remembered once when Edna and I were drunk in Rabbit Town that I stole four dollars from her. She discovered it and said, "Here, you damn thief's my last dollar – take it too," and I did. But more of Edna later.

It became colder and murkier as the day wore on, but I felt glad to be wandering from St. Marys. The horror of the town and of my life there crept over me. The factory whistles every morning, calling men to labour, had always grated on my nerves like files on glass. I saw the many men hurrying to work, carrying battered dinner buckets. I saw girls, with run-down heels and calico dresses going to the woollen mill to work, I thought of my life during all the months – working for three dollars a week and paying two dollars of that for board. It was my bad luck to heat links for a drunken chain-maker and he often missed two and three days a week. Often, my sister, who earned a dollar and a half a week and her board, had given me twenty-five cents to keep my heart from breaking on pay-day. I thought long of my sister.

She had said to me once when she slipped me a quarter, "I don't mind a little bump now and then, Jimmy, but God sure slipped us more than our share!" I recalled the saying and wondered about God, and my heart was filled with a bitterness toward him. But I was an embryo poet, and I had no sense of humour.

I had a brother, Hugh; an ex-jockey, with the eyes of a life-whipped lamb, who could tell verbal tales better than I will ever be able to write them. I grew sentimental about my brother and sister, for I loved them dearly, though I had not bothered to bid them farewell. Anyhow, I would make a lot of money and send it to them. I'd put the whole damn Tully tribe on its feet – I would. Hugh loved horses, so when I made a lot of jack I would have him as my coachman. I had another brother, Tom, killed long since in old Mexico. He died, a skull-cracked adventurer and prospector at twenty-five. He was in Arizona at the time and I wanted to join him but he discouraged me. He wanted me to get an education. I wondered then why that loyal three always wanted me to go to school. I can hear the splendid dead rover still saying, "Jim boy, you're going to get somewhere some day just as sure as God put worms in sour apples. I just know it and I knew it when we were kids in the orphans' home. Don't you never give up, Jim, by God don't you never, you got it in you, and by God you show all the bastards who think the Tullys are a lot o' trash, just because dad was a drunken ditch digger." I thought of the letter he had written me regarding his prospects of finding gold. The postscript was:

"If I win out in this country, Jim, you will share it with me – if I lose I will share it alone."

I thought of Boroff, a maniac farmer who could neither read nor write and for whom I had slaved eighteen months. I recalled the time in Van Wert County when it was twenty-eight degrees below zero and my body had frozen blue because the tiller of the soil would not buy me underwear. I God damned him in my heart and swore under my breath that when I got big enough I would go back there and trounce hell out of him. I glowed with this thought and nursed it as the train rolled along. I wondered why people were so mean to kids. Nearly every kid I knew who had been sent to farmers from the orphanage had run away because they could not stand the treatment. "They're too tight to hire men – the bastards – so they get orphans and work hell out of them." I again thought of Boroff and his daughter Ivy. Neither Ivy nor myself had reached the age of puberty though we had desire for each other. Boroff was a religious fanatic every winter and he would go to revival meetings and often take his half-crazy wife with him, leaving me with Ivy. Alone in the house, Satan would come to tempt us right near the large family Bible. While Boroff sang hosannas to his God I would lie in Ivy's arms. Ivy asked me not to tell, and I didn't, and neither did Ivy. She went to Sunday-school every Sunday and kept her secret well. I often smile when I hear people say that a woman cannot keep a secret.

Ivy was a lovely little girl. Her breasts were as round and hard as apples and her limbs were white as marble. I met her years later and she gave all she had tried to give as a child. But I digress. Women are such fascinating subjects. Ivy had long black hair and sharp and pretty features. Her cheeks glowed red and her breath was hot. She died later of quick consumption.

At one station, after we had finished unloading the freight, a trainman told a smutty story. He used words I did not like, and a revulsion came over me. Strange, down, far down in the gutters where nothing but the sludge and murk of life rolled by, I was never to overcome my revulsion from the filth of it all. If my clothing was lousy I watched clouds sailing across the moon and heard linnets chirping and larks singing.

Even though the dupe of destiny I was a lover of beauty and saw it everywhere. The present adventure clouded all other feelings backward save those of sentiment.

Thinking of all things under the murk-hidden sun, I reached the end of my first journey.

It took all day to make the trip, and we arrived in Muncie from the east at about the time a driving snow storm came from the west. The snow fell steadily for hours, and was driven by the wind in all directions. Finally the wind abated and the snow stopped falling. It became intensely cold. Darkness came. The train crew had long since gone to warm shelter, and supperless, I searched for a warm place, which I found in a sand-shed at the edge of the railroad yards.

The shed was crowded with hoboes. They lolled on boxes, and broken chairs, and in the sand, which was boarded up like loose grain in one-half of the place. A large, round stove was splashed cherry red with the heat. The warmth in the room melted the snow on the roof, and the water dropped through a small space above and fell with a monotonous clatter on a piece of tar-paper in a corner of the sand bin.

Coffee boiled in a granite vessel on top of the stove. Some battered cooking utensils were in a store-box which also contained many varieties of food. There were some small lunches wrapped in paper, which the hoboes called "lumps" and "handouts." These lunches had been given them by kind-hearted people at houses where they had begged.

"Hello, 'Bo," said a derelict, as I entered.

The speaker's mouth sagged at one corner, where a red sear led downward from his lower lip, as though a knife had cut it. He wore a black satine shirt, and a greasy red necktie. His coat was too small for him, and his muscular shoulders had ripped it in the arm-pits.

A decrepit, middle-aged hobo sat near him. He wore a black moustache and several weeks' growth of beard. His collar was yellow and black, and much too large for him. His few remaining teeth were snagged and crooked. A half-dozen other men looked cautiously at me.

After I had greeted them, the first individual spoke again, "She's a tough night, Mate. I come in over the Big Four to-day from Saint Louie. I wanta make it to Cincy an' beat it south."

"I met Frisco Red in Cincy t'other day," said the yellow-collared tramp, "an' he tells me they're horstile down south. Pinchin' ev'ry tramp they see."

"It ain't bad in New Ohleans. A guy kin allus git by there," spoke up another.

"Believe me, 'Boes, I'll pick up a stake in some burg afore I hits it 'way south. Dynamite Eddie's in Chatnoogie. I'll turn a trick wit' 'im, an' stay down there. This God-forsaken jungle is only good for Eskermos."

An engine stopped near the sand-shed. It could be heard puffing in the cold night air. The door was opened, and a man in grease-stained overalls entered with two buckets in which to shovel sand.

"Run outta sand?" asked a hobo.

"Yeah," answered the man in overalls, who looked neither to right nor to left.

"Them engines sure use the sand nights like this," said another hobo.

"Well, they gotta," spoke up the man in the yellow collar. "They'd slide all over the tracks if they didn't."

"Well, we'll let 'em," said another tramp.

The man departed with the sand and soon the engine was heard puffing and straining down the track. Then quiet settled upon the shed in the railroad yards at Muncie. The crackling sputter of the coal in the red-hot stove, and the dropping of the melted snow on the tar-paper was all that broke the silence. The heat made some of the wanderers drowsy, and they stretched out on the sand and snored.

The man with the sagging mouth and the scarred chin offered me food and coffee, which I accepted greedily, as I had not eaten since early morning.

"You ain't been on the road long, Kid," said one shrewd-looking vagabond. "It takes a lotta guts for green kids to beat it on a day like this. I'd beat it back home 'f I was you till the bluebirds whistle in the spring."

Just then the door opened wide and a policeman stood framed in it. His flash-light shone clearly above the blurred light that glimmered through the smudgy globe of the kerosene lantern.

The hoboes in the shed were momentarily alarmed, while I was badly scared, as it was my first contact with the law.

The officer looked about the room, as if in search of a certain individual. "He ain't here, I guess," he said, half aloud to himself, as he held the light in the faces of the group.

"That's all right, men," he continued. "Flop here till mornin' – she's colder'n Billy-be-damned outside."

He sniffed the aroma of the coffee – "Java smells good," he commented, "gimme a cup." The hoboes, anxious to fraternize with so much power, moved in unison to pour the coffee. One of them handed the hot liquid to the policeman, saying as he did so, "Sugar, Mister?"

"Nope," said his blue-coated majesty, "this'll do. Thanks."

The policeman handed back the empty cup, and said, "Lay low here – it's all right."

"Thank you, Mister," replied the grateful tramps in unison.

When the policeman had gone, a hobo said, "Some o' them cops are good guys."

"You gotta watch 'em all," returned another.

The tramps on the sand slept peacefully through it all.

"Them guys could a' been pinched an' they'd never knew it," a vagrant said, as he nodded at the stretched-out forms of the rovers, who breathed heavily. "One time I got stewed in Chi, an' I was thrun outta Hinky Dink's on my ear, and darned 'f I diden sleep right on Clark Street till mornin'."

"That dynamite Hinky Dink sells 'ud make a hummin' bird fly slow," volunteered the man in the yellow collar, and then continued, "I was runnin' for a freight in Pittsy, an' I fell over a switch light, an' got knocked out. She was rainin' cats wi' blue feathers an' green tails, an' I never woke up till mornin, an' I was wetter'n the river. Well, sir, I lays right between the tracks, an' the trains rolled all aroun' me. If I'd a stretched out my arms any they'd o' been on the rails, an' I'd a been a bum wit'out grub-hooks."

He looked down at his grimy hands. His weather-beaten cap sat back on his head, which was smooth all over, and round as a billiard ball. He had no eyebrows. They had gone away with his hair. His eyelids fell away from his eyes and made small gaps, like red wounds, in his face. His rheumy eyes blinked constantly, while his forehead twitched above them nervously.

I watched him with fascinated interest. The man removed his cap and rubbed his rough hand over his smooth head, as though he were placing straggly locks in place.

The tramps laughed outright at the movement, and I joined them. The hairless tramp grinned crookedly as he looked at me.

"Whatsamatter, Red, you jealous?" he asked.

"No, I'd about as soon be red-headed as have no hair at all," I replied.

"Was you born bald-headed?" asked a tramp.

"Nope, I had a fever, an' my hair come out. Some guy tells me to git it shaved an' it'd grow back in quicker."

"Diden it never grow no more atall?" asked a hobo.

"If it ever did, it grew t'other way. I ain't never seen it."

Suddenly there was great commotion outside, and the door was hastily opened. Two flashlights shone in our faces.

"Hands up, everybody," said a rough voice behind one of the lights, as two policemen entered the shed. One of them was the officer who had drunk the coffee. We were lined against the wall and searched.

Our pockets searched, we were marched out of the shed to a spot where two other policemen stood stamping their feet in the snow. Then all four officers marched us to a patrol wagon which stood at the edge of the railroad yards. When we reached the wagon a policeman said, "Jump in," and all obeyed.

The wagon clattered over the rough streets until it reached the police station.

As it lumbered along, one tramp said to me, "You don't remember nothin' anyone said. Get me?"

"Gosh," said one of the men who had lately slept on the sand, "I sure had a good snooze. Dreamt I was eatin' pancakes an' honey."

The wagon drew up at the station and we were marched before the Chief of Police. That austere gentleman scanned us with a disdainful look on his face. "Take 'em away, an' bring 'em in one at a time," he ordered.

We were taken to another room under the guard of two policemen. I was the first to be brought before the Chief, and I walked behind my captor with shaking knees, as though I were on the way to the gallows and had taken a last look at the world.

The Chief's eyes were small, and his face was heavy. He wore a big red moustache, and his whole appearance reminded me of the pictures of brigands I had seen in books of adventure.

"Well," shouted the Chief, as he scowled at me, "what safe did you crack? How long you been out o' jail? Huh!"

I was scared beyond words, and the tears came to my eyes as I looked at the faces of my captors, who stood frowning.

"Talk up, lad, 'fess up. We'll let you off easy if you tell the truth," said the Chief.

I blurted out the truth rapidly.

The Chief's face did not relax. "Did any of that bunch out there say anything about any jobs they'd done, or anything?"

"No, sir," I answered.

"What did they talk about then?"

"Mostly about the weather, and one guy bein' bald-headed, and things."

The questioning over, I was taken to a cell where I remained until all had been questioned and searched again.

Some money was found in the pocket of one of the hoboes and we were taken through the deserted streets to an unpainted, frame building that was barely strong enough to face the winter winds. The policeman rang an old-fashioned doorbell, and presently the door was opened by the most withered old woman I have ever seen.

A garish light streamed behind her. Noticing the policeman, the old woman bowed obsequiously and bent her crooked back almost double.

"Come in, gentlemen,"she said, through teeth-less gums.

The drinker of vagabonds' coffee explained his errand, and gave the old woman the tramp's money, and hurried away with a parting farewell.

"Beat it out of here in the mornin'. If I ketch you 'round here to-morrow night I'll see that you get the Works. Lots o' room in the Work House for vags, you know."

When he had gone, the woman's manner changed at once. Her servile smile disappeared, and hard lines crept around her withered mouth.

She picked up a small kerosene lamp, the globe of which was black with smoke on one side, and said, "Follow me."

She held her gingham checked skirt tight about her fleshless ankles as she walked spryly up the stairs. We followed her until we reached the landing where she showed us many empty beds in an attic dormitory. Two kerosene lamps, fastened by brackets to the wall, burned dimly. The snores of sleeping men broke the silence.

There was but one small window in the attic room. It had four panes of glass, from which the putty had fallen away.

The old hag motioned us to the beds. She then held the lamp over her head and looked about the room. A man moaned in the bed next to me as he tossed uneasily on the mattress. The woman paused for a moment, and looked in the direction of the moaning man. She then turned toward the steps and went creaking down them.

The other sleepers had been undisturbed by our arrival from the street.

I lay awake and wondered what would become of the food which was left in the box. I thought of the one-eyed young tramp I had met so long ago. Many things passed through my mind, but still sleep remained far away as I listened to the whistling of a railroad engine that shrieked through the still night air.

Footsteps were heard on the rickety stairs, and presently the old woman's head appeared above the floor. She held the small lamp in front of her, and walked silently across the floor like a shrunken somnambulist. Two men followed her.

The old woman motioned the men to beds along the wall. Then, holding the lamp above her head, she peered about the room as before. The steps could be heard creaking as she descended them.

The men talked quietly for a few moments until they were ready for bed. One of them looked at the weakly burning lamp on the wall and said half aloud, "I think I'll douse this glim." He walked over to the lamp and held his hand above the globe and smothered the flame.

The room was submjerged in semi-darkness. The other lamp threw dark shadows on the wall at the other end of it.

The man in the bed next to me kept moaning, as though he found it difficult to breathe. "I wonder if he's sick?" I said to myself. I rose from my bed and leaned over him, gazing down into his face, which looked ghastly in the half light. I then walked across to the bed that held the man with the scarred face. He was lying with his hands across his chest, staring up at the ceiling.

"What's wrong, Kid?" he asked.

"I think the guy next to me's awful sick," was my answer.

He jumped out of his bed at once, and found a match in his pocket with which he lit the lamp on the wall near him. He then followed me to the man's cot. His action aroused other vagabonds, who sat up in their beds.

The hobo shook the man's shoulder. "What's a matter, Bloke"? he asked.

"I'm a-l-l in," was the weak reply.

The words travelled over the room, and brought several men from their beds.

"Bring me the glim," commanded the tramp I had aroused.

A vagrant lifted it from the bracket on the wall, and handed it to him.

"Hold this glim, Kid," he told me.

The light streamed over clots of blood on the soiled sheets of the bed. Two men lifted the form of the moaning vagabond, while two other rovers brought pillows and placed them behind him. Then he was gently placed against the pillows in a half-sitting position. "That might keep the red ink from flowin' outta his mouth," said the scarred-face man. Turning to a staring hobo, he said, "Beat it down stairs and tell the old ghost that a guy's dyin' up here. Tell her to send for a croaker." The man hurried down stairs.

The sick man doubled up in a convulsive heap. His ghastly eyes seemed ready to pop out of his head. He coughed so violently that the bed moved under him, as he tore his shirt from his chest in an effort to free his lungs. "Oh, oh, – oh," he moaned.

"They ain't no air in the damn place. Open that window," shouted someone. A tramp hurried to it. "It's nailed shut," he announced. Another tramp hurried to the window with a shoe he had picked from the floor. He knocked out the dirty panes with the heel of it. The jagged glass cut his hand, and in a last blow he let go the shoe and it went hurtling through the broken glass.

"Damn it – there goes my shoe. I'll have to beat it outen the snow after it."

The old woman came stumbling up the stairs. Her withered frame trembled with excitement. The rovers scurried for more clothing as she came.

The faded shawl fell from her shoulders as she stood at the foot of the bed and looked down into the face of the dying man.

"He's croakin'," blurted out a hobo. "Kin you phone a doctor?"

The lamp shook in the old hag's hand. "I have no phone," she answered.

The man groaned louder and louder, and the blood oozed from his mouth, and trickled down the sides of his face, and fell upon his shoulders.

In another moment his frame became rigid. His eyes stared upward, like a thirst-tormented man who beholds a mirage in the desert. Then his arms stretched outward, and his jaws clamped together. There followed a racking spasm of coughing and the jaws clamped again. Then the lips parted in a half-cynical smile. The arms dropped on his chest; the shoulders fell backward. His throat rattled, his chest stopped heaving, and he fell back on the pillow as silent as a stone.

The old woman handed the lamp to a rover standing near her. The death-bed scene stilled every tongue. The woman spoke almost the first words she had uttered to the group of vagabonds. "It's too late for a doctor now" she said, as she placed the sheet over the forever-silent wanderer.

I looked at the sheet which covered the dead man, and then clutched the arm of the hobo with the scarred face.

"It's hell, hey Kid," said that rover. "The old boy's beat the train to the last division."

"Yep," said a tramp onlooker, "no more gettin' ditched, or nothin'."

"It's the man-planter's turn now," said another. "He'll git a hundred bucks fur throwin' him in a pine box."

"Did anyone know him?" asked the old woman. No one answered.

"Where's his rags?" asked the man with the scarred face.

A tramp pulled them out from under the bed. The man with the scarred face searched them. He found a pocket-knife with two broken blades, a nickel, and three pennies. That was all.

"Give the eight cents to the man-planter fur a tip," said a tramp.

"Nope," said the man with the scarred face, "we'll give them to the landlady here." The old lady reached out her withered and crooked hand. The nickel and three pennies fell dully into it. Her fingers closed over them.

"Who was he? Does anyone know?" quavered the old woman.

"Nobody knows, I guess," answered the tramp who had broken the window panes.

"Well, it makes no dif. Who the hell cares 'bout a dead hobo?" said another vagrant.

"Maybe God does," answered the old woman with a hard light in her eyes.

"Maybe He does," said the man who had knocked the glass from the window, "but I'll go and tell the cops, so's they kin take him to the morgue. I gotta git my shoe anyhow outen the street."

Within an hour two policemen came and carried the dead vagabond to a wagon below.

"He gits a free ride in the Black Mariah all to hisself," said a tramp.

Then the dormitory became quiet once again.

CHAPTER III
AMY, THE BEAUTIFUL FAT GIRL

IN FIVE WEEKS IT WAS SPRING.

I left the town in a box car one April morning and hoboed about Kentucky and Indiana for several weeks, and then secured a job with Amy, the Beautiful Fat Girl, whose side-show was the leading attraction with The One and Only Street Fair Company.

Amy weighed nearly five hundred pounds. Her act consisted of dancing upon a heavy glass stage while she held a long piece of white gauze across her shoulders. This was supposed to make her represent an angel. My job was to shift the differently coloured lights upon her as she danced.

An electric light shone under the small stage, which had not room enough under it for me to sit up. In a cramped position, I would shift green, yellow, blue, orange, and many other coloured pieces of isinglass above the light under the stage. The stage and Amy would take on the colour of the glass which I operated. I could hear the applause of the audience as Amy warmed up to her work of looking angelic. Her heavy feet would pound the stage directly above me, and I would always feel relieved when she moved away. Amy had once cracked one of the heavy glass pieces in the stage, and I, of course, hoped for the good of all concerned that she would not fall through it and break the electric globe.

Amy wore rings as large as bracelets. The diamonds in the rings were of many sizes. She had many chins. They ran like the ridges of mountains down to her throat. There was a small red valley between her throat and breasts, which rose like two mountains. They shook as she danced. She was quite the heaviest angel I had ever seen.

Amy drank liquor as no angel had ever drunk it before. Often, when the day's activities were over, she would get gloriously drunk and maudlin. At such times she would forget the strain of being a heavyweight angel and become immensely human.

Her "spieler," as she called him, was not a man who could stand much liquor. He was called Happy Hi Holler, and in street fair circles he was considered the best side show barker in existence. He could have talked a ghost into seeing its shadow. But a few drinks sufficed for Happy Hi Holler. The first drink would make him melancholy, the second would make him sleepy, and the third would make him unconscious.

It was different with me. I was born with the gift of drinking. So, I became Amy's liquor secretary. It was my duty to see that she was always well supplied. This was a task which I found delightful. As the street fair always played a week in each town, and as those were the happy days when bootleggers did not exist, I had no trouble in supplying Amy with many quarts each day. At the end of each week, Amy would give me sixty dollars. This would relieve her of any worry about liquor for another week.

Amy had been a circus freak for years, and, strange to say, she had been a woman with many lovers. Happy Hi Holler had been her sweetheart for over a year, but as he could drink very little, she found, as time went on, that they had less and less in common. Often when John Barleycorn had won another bout with Happy Hi, Amy would tell me of her affairs with men.

A Russian midget had loved her when she was with Barnum, but once in a quarrel, Amy had slapped him a trifle too hard, and almost dislocated his neck. After that Amy had insisted that her lovers be big men. I had learned something about women from those who had lived in Rabbit Town in the red light district of St. Marys. Old Raley had told me of their kindness, and whenever life treated me more harshly than usual, I would tell my troubles to them. All unconciously they had helped me to understand the moods of Amy.

I never knew Amy to frame over three sentences in any conversation. She seldom talked unless asked a question directly, and then her answer was never one of over five words.

However, she liked people who talked, and I was gabbier when drunk than Happy Hi Holler was when sober. I remembered all the doggerel I had ever read, and nearly all the poetry. At that time I could remember almost the exact words of conversations held weeks before.

She had a favourite piece of doggerel, which was nearly endless. Verse after verse it gave in detail the history of one poor girl and her relatives.

> Her pa was sent up for horse stealing,
> Her ma is a pigeon-toed Hun,
> Her sister's a sport in old Wheeling,
> And her brother's a son of a gun.
>
> Her cousin was a drunkard in Cincy,
> He died with a peach of a bun,
> And her uncle's a preacher in Quincy,
> A nutty old son of a gun.

Amy would listen to this doggerel for hours at a time and laugh loudly the while. Her many chins would pucker up as she laughed, and make her face as round as the full moon. Always the quart bottle of liquor was near her.

The seltzer bottle was always near the whiskey. Amy was fond of seltzer and whiskey high-balls. When she became particularly illuminated, she would act quite girlish, and pick up the seltzer bottle and squirt some of its contents in my face. I would join in the laugh, for Amy was my boss, and a generous one besides. I felt that she must have her fun, and though a trifle confused, I would keep on reciting doggerel while the seltzer itched in my eyes, and trickled down my face.

Amy's legs were as big as telephone poles, and her arms were larger than the legs of a big man.

She had all the vanities of her sex. Her cheeks were painted red like ripe Oregon apples all the time. Her shoes were always a size too small for her. She complained constantly about aching feet.

At about this time, one or two of the western states had decided to dispense with liquor. By taking such a drastic step they deprived their citizens of the opportunity of ever witnessing Amy do her angel dance. For Amy refused absolutely to travel with her caravan in dry territory. When I told her the result of one wet and dry election, I heard her speak the longest sentence I had ever heard her utter. "What the hell's the country comin' to?" she asked.

I was later to travel with a great circus through the south, and to wrestle a trick mule with a dog and pony show, but I was never to meet another person quite like Amy. And the parting day was close at hand.

Now, when the night comes down, the immense shadow of the big, free-hearted woman comes before me. She was a pagan with the simplicity of a child. She would swear terribly at me when the strain of her angel dance was upon her. And then, the elephantine woman would pet me when in her cups.

Her voice was as heavy as herself. She was not over thirty-five years old. Her hair was raven black. She combed it straight back from a forehead that sloped directly back from her eyebrows. Her nose was big and flat, and her nostrils were as large as pennies.

All her upper teeth were gold. "Damned nigger dentistry," she called it. She would have no other women about. She seemed to wish nothing to remind her of daintiness, or grace.

The parting came in Sioux City. I was given sixty dollars to get the next week's ration of liquor. I fell in with some other men who had left the Street Fair Company. I became drunk, and was robbed of some of the money. Afraid to face Amy again, I left for Chicago.

I never heard of her again. But I remember. And I wonder if she does. It is not the first time that money has come between friends.

Chapter IV
Adventure Again

WHEN SPRING reached Chicago, it lost me.

I planned a trip to Omaha with a lad of my own age. We left the Northwestern station one night just at dark. Bill had beaten his way on mail trains before.

We waited a few hundred feet from the station, until the train was well on its way. The engine came thundering down the track at a fast rate of speed, and rolled by our hiding place with a great blowing of steam and shrieking of whistle. The engine and first coach were enveloped in white and dark clouds of smoke and steam. We felt our way through the clouds and were soon aboard the train.

My heart beat fast with the thrill of adventure. We reached De Kalb without mishap, and ran for a dark place to hide while the train stopped at the depot. When the engine steamed away, we were aboard the first blind. Another man was there ahead of us.

Great clouds of steam and smoke fell all around us. A faded yellow moon would now and then shine through the vapour. The train ran a few miles until it came to a siding. It stopped for a signal, and was slowly starting up again when the third person spoke. "You guys hold up your hands," he said, as he pointed a long, dark revolver at us.

We did as we were told, and the man hastily handcuffed our wrists together. "We'll ride nice and easy on into Clinton, 'Boes, and I'll see that you get the rock pile for a couple o' months." When the fireman opened the firebox to shovel in coal, a streak of light enveloped the blind baggage.

The man with the gun turned his back on us, and looked out at the passing landscape as the train slowly gained momentum. As he did so, Bill held tightly to the rung of the iron ladder with his free hand, and kicked the majesty of railroad law in the south as he looked north.

The man shot excitedly into the air as he fell from the train. One shot, then several more blazed up at the moon, but the train now sped through the open country at sixty miles an hour.

"Say, Bill, how'll we get these danged handcuffs off?" I asked.

"We'll let a train run over 'em," laughed Bill, and then seriously, "by thunder, we're in a hell of a fix. We'll have to beat it from the train away out from Clinton, 'cause that's where she stops first. That dick-'ll wire on ahead, if he didn't bust his leg or somethin'."

We pulled at the handcuffs. "He sure spliced us easy, didn't he, Bill?" I said.

"Yeah, but he was a mail order dick at that – 'cause a good detective don't turn his back on a guy."

The wind swept around the train and blew smoke and steam-blended clouds across the Illinois fields.

Our minds were busy with the immediate problem ahead – that of getting off a hastily moving train while handcuffed together. We both felt that to leave the train the minute the whistle blew for the yards at Clinton was the only safe thing to do.

We resolved to take any chance rather than be arrested for attacking an officer. Bill talked over details with me, and I said, "It'd be a devil of a note, if we got hurt an' pinched, too."

"Columbus took a chance, an' he didn't have jail starin' him in the mug, either," blurted Bill.

Within an hour the engine whistle blew for the yards at Clinton. "Maybe the dick ain't got to a telegraph yet, but we better not ride on, anyhow," said Bill.

The train slowed up a trifle as we climbed down on the one iron step attached to the car. We looked at the ground that seemed to be rolling swiftly with the train. "We can't make it yet," shouted Bill, while he touched his foot on the ground as if to test the speed. "We'd break our rough necks." There was a nervous silence for some moments. "Now, when you jump, Red, be sure you're clear of the train. Don't get your foot caught, for God's sake. I don't wanta die with you. Throw yourself when I do,'" commanded Bill.

"Be sure and pick a soft place to land, Bill," I suggested.

"Any place's softer'n jail, old boy. We'd better beat it now. We're sure to roll away from the train on this bank. That'll beat rollin' under. We'll soon be in the yards now."

We held to the train with our shackled hands. Bill had me take the position furthest from the car so that chances of a mishap would be lessened.

"Now, when I count three, let go," yelled Bill. "One—two—" We came to a bridge which crossed a body of water. On the other side Bill yelled, "Three," and we let go of the train simultaneously. Somehow I fell and dragged Bill with me. He soon had me sitting upright. The handcuffs had torn the flesh from our wrists. Otherwise we were unhurt.

We walked along the bank of the Mississippi river, and hunted for two heavy rocks under the blurred light of the moon.

"We'll lay our mitts on one rock, and I'll crack the handcuffs with the other rock," suggested Bill.

"That suits me," I replied.

We found a flat rock imbedded in the earth, and after another search, a smaller rock was found.

Bill used the smaller rock as a hammer. He became excited once, and missed the handcuff, and hit my wrist. "Hey, you cock-eyed boob, watch what you're doin'," I yelled.

"Well, you hit 'em then," suggested Bill.

I took the rock and pounded the irons until they spread and broke. We moved our free wrists again and laughed like children.

Bill took the broken handcuffs and tossed them into the river. They fell into the water with a loud plunking sound.

"Hope a carp eats 'em for bait," said Bill, as he looked at the river. "I got an idea," he continued, "we'll get a job in vaudeville, Houdini an' Kellar, the handcuff kings."

"We better watch out, Bill. We ain't outta this burg, yet."

"All we have to do's lay low. They never pinch the right tramp when anything's done. They just pinches the first guy they sees and says to themself, 'Well, he's a tramp, anyhow, an' we'll stick 'im up for sixty days,'" said Bill.

"I know, but it'd be tough for a couple o' guys to be sent up for what we done," I said.

"It's all'n the game, Red. When you're on the bum long enough someone'll stick you up for somethin' some other guy done. The big trick's don't let 'em ketch you."

Bill was from the reform school at Pontiac, Illinois. He had served two terms, the first term for vagrancy, and the second for cutting a negro with a knife.

Bill had blond hair, and a sharp face. He had blue eyes, a straight nose, and a square chin. He was a heavy-set youth, and his shoulders were broad and powerful. He had no morals at all, and was as irresponsible as the wind. He had two fine traits, being free-hearted and cheerful always. He never thought of himself first, whether it was the sharing of a dollar, or a slice of bread. His bodily cleanliness amounted to a passion. He was quick in movement and daring in resolve.

We walked along the Mississippi for some time without speaking. Then Bill said, "I'll tell you, Red, I'll stick a knife in any dick that tries to catch me before I spend all summer in jail."

"Sure thing," I replied, "only a guy's safer bustin' 'em in the jaw, or kickin' 'em off a train."

"Maybe you're right," returned Bill, "but the next guy that sticks me in jail's got a battle on his hands. I been in jail five years. That's enough."

We came to an old flat-boat that rose and fell with the waves. We walked out to it on a board that stretched from the bank. With coats over our shoulders and our shoes for pillows, we watched the stars and listened to the lapping of the waves against the boat until we fell asleep.

The sun climbed early over a wood nearby and threw its rays up on our faces. We sat erect and sleepily watched the peaceful scene around us. Some geese were swimming in circles in the middle of the river. A passenger train thundered over the railroad bridge on its way to Chicago. The frogs still croaked along the bank as we left the boat.

We walked away from the railroad tracks for several hundred feet. Smoke curled through the air at the edge of a wood. As we drew near, we smelt the odour of frying meat and boiling coffee.

Five hoboes sat around the fire, Indian fashion. Another stood above the fire and turned meat in an immense iron skillet. The men looked at each other as we approached. The tramps were quickly put at their ease as soon as Bill had spoken a few words to them.

A box-car door was laid upon some railroad ties to serve as a table. Some battered tin dishes were upon it.

The man who cooked the food was a tall angular hobo, with an eagle face that wore a constant sneer. His nature was as cold as though ice had frozen about his heart. He did not speak to us at all. A bleared, one-armed man, with heavy body, and heavier stomach rose from his seat. He stood in front of us, and asked, "You kids runaways?"

"Nope, you got us wrong. We ain't got nothin' to run away from."

"Hey, Lanky," yelled the one-armed tramp to the cook, "Kin these kids eat?"

"Are they broke?" asked another tramp, when Lanky ignored the question.

"We're flatter'n feet wit' broken arches," replied Bill.

"Come an' eat then," said the one-armed man.

A breeze came up and swayed the tops of the trees in the woods. The sun threw leafy shadows across the car-door table. The greed of hungry men was the only thing that spoiled the scene. Birds darted over the landscape and flew low across the broad river. The geese swam leisurely in the direction of the tramps.

The one-armed man looked up from his food and noticed the handsome buff-colored goose that swam in the lead. He spoke aloud as if in warning to the goose, "Come aroun' to-night, old feller, an' we'll make a stew outta yu."

The men talked but little at first, but when their hunger was appeased, the conversation became livelier. Even Lanky, the cook, was moved to speak once or twice.

"Which way you kids come from?" asked one of the men.

"From Chi," answered Bill.

"Where you goin'?" asked another.

"Just driftin' around for the summer," I answered.

"I beat it through De Kalb last night on the rods of a manerfest meat train, an' I hears 'em. talkin' in the yards 'bout some dick 'at got kicked off Number One."

"This country'll be hostile now," said the one-armed man. "Clinton allus was a tough town for the 'boes. Maybe we'd better mooch on outta here."

"We will like the devil," spoke up another tramp. "If any dick comes 'round here, we'll make 'im swim like one o' them geese. We'll make 'im gurgle water like a crab."

The one-armed man left the table and settled himself under the shade of a large white-oak tree. He deftly filled a corncob pipe with his one hand, and lit the match quickly by the twist of his thumb nail, and in another moment was the picture of solid contentment.

I stretched out upon the ground near the one-armed man, and lost myself in the contents of the magazines scattered under the tree. Bill soon walked over toward us. He lingered for a few minutes, but being unable to stay long in one place, he soon rose and walked about through the woods. In a short time, he returned, carrying a broomstick, which he laughingly twirled as a cane.

The hoboes scattered within an hour and returned to camp late in the afternoon. They were heavily laden with food which they had bought and begged.

Bill begged eighty cents on the main street of Clinton, and I begged fifty cents from a red-faced man who was drunk. The man was moved by the tragic story which I told, and he took me into a nearby saloon with him. Bill, who was begging on the other side of the street, was quick to size up the situation, and followed us into the saloon.

I introduced Bill at once, without giving the man a name. He shook hands with Bill and invited him to drink also. The bartender became interested in the tales of tramping we told, and when we left, he gave each of us a pint of whiskey. So with a dollar and thirty cents and two pints of red-eye between us, and with our heads teeming with liquor, we headed for the hobo camp.

It was mid-afternoon when we arrived at the camp, and contributed the liquor as our share of the day's spoils. The angular hobo cook smiled crookedly as he saw the red fluid in the bottles. He quickly opened the first one, saying, "You kids're dern good moochers." The whiskey rattled down his boney throat, until another tramp grabbed the bottle from him. "What you t'ink it is, your birt 'day, Lanky?" he sneered.

The tramp held the bottle up so all could see. Lanky had drained a half pint of it. "We got a pint an' a half o' this now, an' I got a pint o' gin, and there's six oranges here a grocery guy give me. So I'll boil a couple a gallons o' water, and pound the oranges in it, and mix up the gin and red-eye. That'll give us some highballs. You guys willin'?"

All consented, and the tramp soon busied himself mixing the strange concoction. "You oughta put some ker-sene in it," suggested another tramp.

"I'll put some rough-on-rats in it for Lanky," volunteered the mixer.

The concoction was ready in a short time, and the rovers drank it out of dented tin cups made rusty by the rain.

Forgetful of the law, and of wasted lives, the men were soon singing ribald hobo songs that would have delighted Rabelais. They sang a song which contained many verses. The hero went through all the adventure of a hobo Don Juan, and at last ended in peace and quiet, and this part of his career can be printed:

HE SETTLED DOWN

Where the cigarettes grow near the lemonade springs,
In the big potato mountains.
Where the ham an' eggs grow on trees,
And bread grows from the ground,
An' the springs squirt booze to your knees,
An' there's more than enough to go 'round.
Where the chickens crawl into the skillet,
An' cook 'emselves up nice an' brown,
An' the cows churn their butter'n the mornin',
An' squirt their milk all aroun'.
Where the lunches grow on the bushes,
And bump the 'boes in the eyes,
An' every night at eleven,
The sky rains down apple pies.

So Iowa Slim sits on his porch,
While his wives all play wit' his hair – ,
And he sees the freight trains runnin',
An' he says, "Go on, I don't care."

For he was an old-time floater,
An' he had more wives than a priest,
An' each of them loved the ol' bloater –
The dirty ol' bum of a beast.

His home is where the bird sings,
And young girls swim in the fountains,
An' the cigarettes grow with the matches,
In the big potato mountains.

The sun went down while the men laughed and sang, and twilight touched the edge of the woods. It softened even the features of the men at the camp. Crickets and frogs set up a dismal singing. "I'm three sheets in the wind," said Bill, as he twirled his broom-stick deftly in his hand.

A husky tramp lit a battered lantern and placed it on the car-door table. "If some guy gets some more wood, I'll start cookin' some chuck," he said. "Lanky needs a rest." Lanky was stretched out on the grass. Three hoboes started to gather wood at once. One of them could be heard singing in the woods as he picked up the pieces.

Two other men turned from the river and joined the tramps at the fire. They looked like hoboes in the indistinct light. The tramps at the fire spoke cautiously, not feeling certain of the identity of the callers. One of the men stood near Bill for a moment, and then stepped back further. Bill stepped back with him. The second man walked easily over to the other side, and stood at the far edge of the crowd near the husky hobo who had just placed a kettle of water on the fire. "Hurry up wit' that wood, you guys," yelled the husky hobo.

The man near Bill covered the crowd with a gun and said sharply, "Up with your hands; you're pinched." A tramp kicked the lantern over. The detective turned slightly in confusion. Bill crashed the broom-stick across the wrist of the man, and the revolver fell to the ground as he shrieked. The thudding of a heavy fist was heard across from Bill. A body fell suddenly and lay quiet.

The men returned with the wood, and instantly took in the situation and dropped it hastily. A man picked up the gun from where it had fallen, while Bill and another vagabond knocked the attempted user of it to the ground, and kicked him fiercely.

The one-armed tramp spoke up. "Search 'em. Maybe they're yeggs, an' ain't dicks."

The men were searched and two pairs of handcuffs were found on them. Bill spoke softly to me. "This is the same guy I kicked off the rattler last night," he said.

"I know it," I whispered back.

"Well, what'll we do wit' 'em?" asked the husky tramp.

"Feed 'em to the fish, if they'll eat 'em," said Lanky, who was awakened by the confusion.

The detective who had been hit by the husky tramp lay moaning on his back. "I socked 'im jist like I hits a boiler with a sledge," said the husky man. "When I slam 'em, they fall, believe me."

"You sure you didn't break his jaw?" asked Lanky.

The husky hobo leaned down and worked the man's jaws sideways with his hands. "Nope, they ain't broke. They just sag a little," said he.

"Throw that gat in the river," commanded the one-armed vagrant to the man who had picked up the gun. "Don't get caught wit' it on you."

"I'll take a chance, an' pawn it. She's wort' twenty-five smacks."

"All right, you're the doctor, but I don't travel wit' no guy that's got a gat, not through this hostile diggin's," was the terse response.

"Let's handcuff 'em to the trees an' beat it," suggested the husky individual. You're goin' to Chi, Lanky, you kin writer the Chief o' p'lice a card an' tell 'em where they are. That's more'n they'd do for us."

The two helpless officers were dragged to trees about ten inches in diameter. Unconscious still, they were seated in upright positions against the trees, with their wrists handcuffed on the other side.

When this was done, the one-armed man said, "Now let's beat it outta here. We kin get Number One west, afor' these guys come to.

They'll be no one at the depot now when she pulls in. The dicks'll be detained on important business elsewhere. Ha, ha, ha."

All left for the depot but Lanky, who walked to the eastern end of the yards and waited for a freight bound for Chicago.

An hour later seven of us rode Number One out of Clinton.

Chapter V
A Tale of the Philippines

FOUR OF THE MEN left the mail train at Cedar Rapids. Bill and I rode on to Boone with the one-armed man. Having a small amount of money, we purchased food and took it to a hobo camp, where we remained until late afternoon before boarding a freight train for the west.

The crew saw us climb into an empty box car as the train left the yards, but did not molest us. As it rolled slowly along the tracks, we made ourselves comfortable for the one hundred and forty miles to Omaha.

We travelled about ten miles across a high viaduct that spanned a great chasm below. Standing at the door of the car, we watched the smoke from the engine curl in black clouds above the green trees that resembled bushes at the bottom of a canyon. Wind-swayed, the trees undulated like the waves of a green ocean.

The train stopped on the western end of the viaduct and the entire crew came to the box car and attempted to collect money from us. "Pay us, or hit the gravel," snarled the conductor.

"We ain't got nothin'," said the one-armed man. "Besides, don't you guys get your wages from the road? Why take a tramp's money?"

"Never mind that. We ain't haulin' live stock," answered a brakeman.

Realizing that an open fight would do no good because the train crew was armed, we crawled out of the car.

The conductor, in an effort to collect a smaller amount, said, "Come on, we'll let you ride for a buck apiece. Three dollars ain't too much."

"Nope," answered Bill, "I wouldn't give you a cent if you hauled me cheap as a letter. It's against my principles."

"How about you, Red?" asked a brakeman.

"Do you know what the Pope told the Cardinal?" I asked in reply.

"Nope, – What?"

"To go to hell," I answered.

The crew's quest for vagabonds' riches, ended, a brakeman stood near with a gun while the rest of the men went to their posts. Then the train slowly pulled out, and we watched it merge into distance.

We walked to a shanty at the end of the viaduct where a man sat in the door whittling a green stick of wood.

He was about thirty-three years old, with flabby face, black eyes, and flat nose. He wore an army hat, which sat jauntily on the back of his head. His shirt was open, and disclosed an American flag tattooed on his chest.

"How far's it back to Boone?" Bill asked.

The man looked up from his whittling and answered tersely, "'Bout ten miles."

"How far's it to a town t'other way?" asked the one-armed man.

"'Bout twenty to where a train stops," answered the man with the flag on his chest.

"Well," said Bill, "let's hike across this bridge to Boone."

"You can't do that, Mates. That's what I'm here for – to let no one cross. Train caught a guy out there in the middle one time, an' bumped him down in them trees like a dead bird," said the flag-chested man as he resumed whittling.

We stood silent for a moment, and he continued, looking up, "A train slows up here to-night, and you might be able to make the rods out on her. She's a meat run, and travels fast as a mail train. All sealed cars. You might as well stay here, because you'd have to walk five miles so's to cross an' hit the pike for Boone, and then you'd have ten or twelve miles by road." It was easy to be seen that the man was lonely.

The sun soon sank, and the sky faded to a dull grey. Then a blood red cloudy line appeared along the horizon, and grey clouds, resembling cement castles with turrets, rested upon it. Yellow clouds rolled above the castles, like immense butterflies unable to find a bush upon which to light.

In a short time all turned scarlet, then purple black, then mauve. At last, dark shadows crept over the earth, and all the colours merged into blue, through which the stars shone.

Fascinated by the scene, I watched silently while the three others talked of nothings.

Hoot owls began calling to each other down below in the trees. A dog could be heard barking ever so far away.

"These nights remind me of the Philippines," said the watchman.

"You been in the Islands?" asked the one-armed man.

"I sure have," replied the watchman. "Three years."

"Gosh, so was I," said the one-armed man,

"Lose your arm over there?" asked the watchman.

"Yep, but not for my country, for a girl." No one else spoke, and the one-armed hobo continued:

"A guy don't get the right kind of girls in this country. They're all corn-fed. This little girl I knew was part Bagobo, part Filipino, and the other half Chinese. She was as purty as ham and eggs to a bum. She belonged to the Mestizoz; they're the Jews of the Island." The watchman nodded. "This little girl was a darb, and I was nuts about her. Her dad was a Chink and owned a gamblin' house. She used to love me too, and Lordy, – how she could love. She was only sixteen, as they come women early in that country. Her mother's people were Bagobos. The Mestizoz won't fight; they're too busy collectin' interest to fight. But the Bagobos'll fight, and they can ride like Indians, and carry spears when they battle. They keep records of their horses for years, and they love them like the Arabs.

"One time this little girl's dad give her ten bucks. She bought a lot of sugar with it, and then sent a lot of servants outen the woods to gather guavas. She made the cook make the jelly and then she had the servants peddle it. She made a bunch o' dough this way, and then she went to tradin' jewellery. She got an iron safe, and put a lot of pearls and diamonds in it. She cheated like sin. I was sittin' purty on top of the world with four diamonds she give me. She sure knew how to make dough, and mind you, she was only sixteen.

"You know where the Diga river is?" asked the speaker of the watchman.

The latter answered, "Yep" as he filled his. pipe and lit it.

"Well, this was at a town called Vera. The country all around is danged purty. The women can ride horses like the men, and you ought to have seen that little blackheaded girl of mine ride. Sometimes I've a notion to go back. But maybe she's fat and ugly now. I know I am, but I didn't use to be.

"Her dad wanted to send her away to Spain to educate her, as a lot of them are sent everywhere to school. They always come back to the old life just like the Indians. It's just as good as ours at that, as all people like us do is work. I don't.

"My girl had a brother who was a priest, and darn smart. Her old man was a Christian when he was younger, then he turned to the Chink religion again. Lots of them turn Christian till they get a pile of money.

"Well, the old heathen suspicioned me likin' his girl, so one time he give a big dinner on New Year's day. It's in Feb'uary over there, and they hold a week's holiday and have roast pig and all the fixin's.

"I got stewed on some green booze that would tear the hide off a mule. So they called an old Chink doctor, and he explained a lot of junk to me, and felt my pulse on the bridge of my nose. Then someone busted me on the head and a lot of drunken Chinks and half-breeds started fightin' with me. They got me in a corner an' I had to fight like a Mick at Donnybrook Fair. My little girl kept screamin' and tryin' to get to me, but a Chink pulled her back every time. Another Chink come runnin' at me with a crooked knife and I picked up a chair and jabbed it at him. He come a tearin' in anyhow, and I upper-cut him and stood him right on his wig, and he twirled around like a top. Some other Chinks got at me after I dropped a couple more. I was darn near all in myself, but I shot out my arm at a half-breed and another guy zipped it off with a long crooked knife. The blood spurted, an' my girl got away and run to me, and some other Chink grabbed her, while her old dad stood back shoutin' orders not to kill me, as that would of got him in hot water.

"I darn near bled to death, but the old Chink doctor stopped the blood, while I slept like a baby through it all.

"My three years was up in the Army in four months, and by that time my arm was all well, so they shipped me back to Frisco on a transport. The Chinks shipped the little girl away somewheres, as I never saw her after the fight."

He paused, and felt his empty sleeve, and resumed, "I came near gettin' the guard house, but the Captain wasn't a bad guy and I guess he thought losin' an arm was bad enough after losin' such a purty little gal. The Captain was a good judge of woman flesh, so he let me down easy. Anyhow, I think I'll beat it to Frisco and ship over there and look around."

"She must have been a peach," said the watchman. "I used to have a good lookin' little trick in Manila, and I often think about her. I've got a wife and three kids over in Boone now, but I wish to thunder I was a single guy again. Damned if I don't. To hell with married life."

A yellow meat train thundered across the viaduct, as though carrying supplies to a starving army.

All four stood up. "This train'll run fifty miles without a stop," said the watchman. "If you make her outta here, you're good for that far anyhow."

A man waved a lantern from the caboose, and then disappeared inside.

With a hasty, "So long," to the watchman, and, "Good luck," in return, we boarded the train.

CHAPTER VI
A RIVER BAPTISM

WE REACHED OMAHA in the early morning. The one-armed man went on to San Francisco, bound for the Philippine Islands where his dream woman lived. We stayed with him until he boarded a Union Pacific freight for the west.

As tramps' minds veer quickly, we suddenly decided to go to St. Louis. A drifter in Omaha had told us that wages were high in the harvest fields near there. We wanted the wages of course, but we did not care much about the work.

A swift ride on a mail train found us on the levee front of a small town near St. Louis by the afternoon of the next day, which was Sunday.

A throng of negroes chanted hymns in a half circle near the river. A negro preacher with a heavy paunch, a lame leg, and a bullet head, stood on the bank of the Mississippi, which they faced. He kept time with a song book, which was held in both hands. As his hands made the downward motion they struck a heavy watch chain from which dangled two large charms attached to the ends of a brass horse shoe.

As we approached the gathering in the company of a derelict we had met, the words of the song became more distinct:

"O, de joy dat fills de moment.
O, de happiness I know,
Seek no longer to detain me – "

and then in voices of thunder accompanied by wild movements,

"Loose de cable – le-t m-e g-o."

This was followed by shouting and the clapping of hands, and verses of another song –

"It's de old time religion,
It's de old time religion,
It's de old time religion –
An' it's good enough for me.

It was good for our old mammy,
It was good for our old mammy,
It was good for our old daddy,
An' it's good enough for me.

It makes de Methodis lube the Baptis'
It makes de Methodis lube the Baptis',
It makes de Methodis lube the Baptis',
An' it's good enough for me."

At the ending of the song, two ropes were fastened to posts in the bank. A negro then waded out into the yellow river about twenty feet and fastened the other ends of the ropes to two poles which projected out of the water. When he had finished, the ropes were stretched a couple of feet above the water.

The preacher then laid his vest on the bank and grasping the ropes with heavy dark hands, he waded into the river. His feet slipped in the soil beneath, and the ropes swayed and bent as the water rolled over his head. He struggled upward while his congregation sang loudly:

"Shall we meet in dat blest harboh
When ouh stohmy trip is o'er,
Wheah St. Peter'll hold ouh ancoh,
On the fah celestal shoah.

Shall we meet wit' Christ ouh Sabior,
When He comes to claim His own,
When He gibes the black folks fabour,
All about His golden throne."

By this time the minister had gained his footing, and was waving his right hand for one of the faithful to follow him. At last the preacher reached the end of the ropes and stood with his back to the river, facing the crowd. One by one the members of the congregation walked out and were held under the water while the crowd on the shore shouted and sang.

In the crowd, was an unbeliever, who made fun of the members of his race. One old lady struggled back to the shore after her immersion and shouted. "I'se washt in de blood o' the Lamb. I'se pure."

"You may be puah, sistah," said the unbeliever, "but you ain't sanitary."

But unmindful of the taunt, the old lady shouted,

"Oh, oh, the Lawd give de worl' to me,
Tomorrer He'll gimme de heabens, and den He'll
gimme de sea,
An' battleships all lined with gold
Shall sail to the peahly gate.
Oh, oh, I'se glad I'm old –
For I hain't much moah to wait."

"Come on sinnehs. Come on sinnehs. De Lawd am you' tabenackle," she shouted.

"Some o' dese sinnehs heah bettah git the walls o' dere tabenackle washed down, 'cause they's awful dihty," laughed the unbeliever.

She started singing, and as the preacher caught up the words, all joined in,

"Whiteh than snow, yes whiteh than snow,
Now wash me an' I shall be whiteh than snow."

"It 'ud take a devil of a lot of washin' to make them whiter'n snow," laughed Bill.

The more they sang, the more hysterical they became. Some of them attempted to fly from the ground, like immense black crows with wings. They fell and rolled on the earth. An old black woman with yellow teeth refused to go in the water, as she said it was too cold.

"The Lawd knows neitheh cold noh hot," shouted the preacher.

"I does though, an' ah don't wanta ketch my deat' o' cold," she answered. "I ain't ready to meet im' yet."

The sun had slanted far westward long before the black children had all been immersed in the yellow water. The preacher, perspiring from the effort of holding the hysterical religionists in the river, surveyed with tired eyes those who remained. There were seven others yet to partake of the holy sacrament. Two more waded out to the minister, while the members on the shore sang fervently as ever.

The preacher's vest lay huddled up near the bank, completely unnoticed by all but Bill and myself.

"I'm goin' to cop the vest," said Bill. "There's a turnip in it, and chain."

The congregation sang lustily as the last three waded to the tired baptizer of the flock. Bill picked up the vest, saying, "I'll meet you guys at the edge of the yards an hour from now."

"All right," we returned.

As Bill disappeared, the derelict with me said, "That guy'll git by all right. Now who'd a thought about gittin' that vest?"

When the last sinner was dipped into the water, a happy shout went up from the dark assemblage. Even the cynical unbeliever was touched. His smile of ridicule was gone, and he was quite humble. "Brethren," he said to those around him, "I wish to join in this happy 'casion. I feels de workin's ob de Lawd wit'in me." He shouted lustily as he clambered out to the weary preacher who leaned on a post at the end of the rope.

The unbeliever was duly immersed amid the laughter, shouting, and tears of the dripping-wet negroes on the shore.

The heavy minister, his clothes clinging tightly to his body, then made for the shore, while the audience sang,

> "Yes, we'll gatheh at the riber,
> The beautiful, the beautiful riber,
> Gat-her wit' de saints at the riber,
> That flows by de throne of Gawd.

> "On de margin ob de riber,
> Washin' up its silber spray,
> We will walk an' talk foreber,
> All de happy golden day."

By this time the minister had reached the shore. His mind at once turned to earthly things, and a startled look came into his eyes as he glanced at the spot where his vest had once been.

"Any de brudders an' sistehs see mah vest?" he shouted.

"Yes – we did. It was right theah." All looked incredulously at the bare ground.

"The Lawd won't forgive sich a action as that," said the minister with little faith in his flock. "He who steals de clothin' of the workeh in the vineyahd shall be damned to everlastin' fi-ah," he shouted. "De watch de congragation gimme an' some money de crowd gives me was in theah too, an' fohteen dollahs o' my own. Look about you brud-ders. Look about you sistehs. Maybe it am mislaid."

"It's mislaid all right," said my derelict companion.

The minister and his flock looked about as though not believing their own eyes. The heavy shepherd of dark sheep walked back again and again to the spot where the vest had once been. "It ain't theah," he murmured. "It suah ain't theah." Then turning to me, he asked, "You no see a vest did you, boy?"

"I did," I truthfully answered, "But I don't now."

"No, I don't nuther, " replied the minister.

The members looked at one another with questioning eyes. "Suahly no one would take de clothin' of the Lawd's sheph' d. Suahly not," moaned the minister.

"Maybe a dog carried it off," suggested a dripping woman.

"Yes, I saw a big dog here a half hour ago. It had a rag, or some-thin' in its mouth. I remember now," lied the vagrant with me.

"Which way did it go?" asked several members at once.

"Down that way," he answered, indicating a direction the other way from which Bill had gone.

The weary members of the baptismal party left at once in the direction the imaginary dog had gone.

They merged into the darkness, talking excitedly, while we hurried to find Bill.

That rover was stretched out in some grass at the edge of the rail-road yards.

"Let's beat it to East St. Louis," he said. "We kin get a drink over there. It's open on Sunday."

The three of us hurried to a street car, and were soon in a saloon with drinks in front of us.

What did you do with the vest?" I asked.

"I threw it in the river. It needed baptizin'," answered Bill, as he looked at a heavy gold watch. "I got thirty-eight bucks altogether," he went on. "I'll give you five," and he handed a bill to the derelict, "and we go fifty-fifty on the rest, Red."

The drinks flowed fast, and the derelict became loquacious. He showed us a letter from a jailor in Georgia. The letter stated that the bearer had served eleven months and twenty-nine days with credit, and that, though the bearer had been sentenced for vagrancy, he had proven an admirable worker at all tasks. The derelict was as proud of it as more fortunate men are of degrees which amount to no more.

Within a few days, we were broke again. The rover from the prison in Georgia had left us quite suddenly on the first night. Bill had sent him to a pawnbroker with the hope that he would bring back money for the watch. Bill had a motive.

"A fellow always takes a chance to get nabbed soakin' some other guy's watch," said Bill, as the derelict departed with the time-piece.

"You're takin' just as big a chance sendin' that guy with it," I returned. He was.

The rover never came back.

CHAPTER VII
FURTHER ESCAPADE

WE DRIFTED, PENNILESS, about the country for some time, and finally went to work for a farmer called Mabee. We each drove an aged team hitched to a decrepit wagon, which creaked noisily down the road. The harness on our teams was held together by wire and ropes.

We had a bed in the hay-loft above the horses. Rats could be heard scampering about during the still hours of the night, and now and then a bat would fly into the large open space in the loft, and circle swiftly about, squeaking like a rat on wings.

We heard that if a bat once fastened itself on the human body it could not be removed without the help of a razor, and the loss of the flesh upon which it had alighted, so we would cover ourselves with the blankets until the bat had found the open space again.

Mosquitoes would leave their headquarters near a stagnant pond in search of blood. Their melancholy buzz could be heard throughout the night. They seemed to drill through the blankets, for all parts of our bodies would be swollen from their bites each morning.

Now and then numbers of lightning bugs would fly into the loft and circle about. Sometimes, when their lights would flare simultaneously, the place would be lit up enough to enable us to distinguish objects within.

Mr. Mabee was the father of a daughter whom we never succeeded in meeting face to face. She was always in retreat when we drew near. It became a joke between us – and we used to say each morning, "Well, maybe you'll see Miss Mabee today, and maybe you won't." The nearest we ever came to seeing her was one morning when she had been late setting the breakfast table. We suddenly came into the room in time to see her form going out of the door into the kitchen.

Mrs. Mabee would wait upon the table. She had either been born tired, or became tired soon after birth. No woman could have become so tired without years of experience.

Her face was sallow; her cheeks hollow. It seemed a mighty effort of feeble will for her to keep her eyes open. She would stand near us with a green bush in her hand and move it slowly across the table with the possible intention of keeping the flies away. She failed. The flies would merely light upon the bush and rest their wings until they came nearer to the butter. They would then leave the bush and drop into it.

Mr. Mabee seldom, if ever, talked. He was as tired as his wife.

When Mr. Mabee's harvesting was done, he helped other farmers for miles around. Or, to put it more precisely, we did.

When the work was done, we would sit on the rickety wagons and hold the lines while the tired horses stumbled tiredly home. We became attached to our teams and were as kind to them as possible. Mr. Mabee would always have the hay and grain ready for them, but after he had gone into the house, we would give them a more generous supply. We could hear the horses munching late into the night, and, somehow, we always enjoyed listening to the noise they made.

There was no social life for us in the country. The snobbery which permeates the American Republic was always in evidence. There was a girl our own age at one farm, who became almost friendly with us. But her horrified mother soon put a stop to her natural impulse of kindness. "Come away from them hoboes," she commanded. Her daughter obeyed.

We soon left our employer, and were given twenty-four dollars each for our labor. The farmer did not even grunt us a farewell, and neither did the tired woman appear in the doorway as we walked down the road toward the railroad track.

Being always too sentimental for a hobo or a business man, I petted the two decrepit horses before I left. Bill followed my example with his team. The poor horses, galled from the rubbing of the wretched, sweat-stained harness, were possibly losing the best friends they ever had. The human animal must bestow its affection on something, and we had whiled away hours with them.

There followed several days of riotous living in St. Louis. The money for which we had laboured two weeks was soon all gone but a few dollars before we decided to take to the road again. This we did with no remorse.

We left the railroad yards at St. Louis on a freight train with two other men who had never beaten their way before.

All four of us were half drunk. The two men had no money, but they did have two quarts of liquor between them, which their last cent had bought.

We were in an empty coal car. Papers were strewn on the floor of the gondola, across which a heavy wire was stretched in the form of a hammock.

Becoming maudlin with drink, we sat on the wire and sang all the songs we could remember. A brakeman came across the train and stopped in the car with us. He proved to be, in the parlance of the road, a "boomer," a sort of hobo, or migratory railroad worker. He joined us in a drink, and went on his way across the train. But the gondola had an attraction for him, and he returned quite often.

As the train neared B———, a railroad division, the brakeman warned us that the town was "hostile."

"This whole country's hostile now since they found them two guys beat up an' handcuffed to trees over in C———. Better not ride into the yards, but git off outside and walk on through. The dick don't come on till 'bout eight o'clock, an' you kin beat it through and have a feed an' be at the other end o' the yards before that."

We left the train as the engine whistled for the yards. It was still travelling rapidly, and Bill and I jumped first, and ran with the train, thus keeping upright without falling.

The two other rovers left the car suddenly and rolled down the steep embankment. We helped them brush the dirt out of their clothing and hair.

We walked to a railroad restaurant where a boomer waiter took our order.

"She's a hostile burg," said the waiter. "This dick here 'ud pinch his mother if she walked on railroad property. He's a Mick, an' he talks with a brogue as thick as butter. But he don't come around this early, hardly ever. You got time to scoff and beat it down the track 'afore he does."

The meal took all but a few cents of our money. The four of us walked down the tracks directly through the yards.

We had not gone many rods, when a man stepped out from between two cars. The moon was just rising above the horizon. Its light was still weak, and the earth was shrouded in almost complete darkness. Some red and green signal lights burned in the yards and made the tops of the steel rails shine a grayish white.

"Where ye goin?" asked the man as he flashed a light in our faces.

"I'm going to Chicago, Mister, to my father," I lied quickly. "He's sick in a hospital there, and I've been workin' in the harvest fields up the line to send him money."

The man searched me, a blackjack hanging from his wrist as he did so. Bill stepped up next and told his story. He had been working with me, and he was helping me get home. "Uh huh," grunted the man.

Then turning to the other two, "Where ye from?" The men answered haltingly. They were more honest than we, but still, the detective did not believe their stories as readily.

"Well, come on," said he. "Ye kin tell your tales to the judge in the mornin'."

He placed two of us on each side of him, and we walked down the tracks.

There was no chance to talk, but Bill and I did some rapid thinking. We each decided that the detective had neither handcuffs nor revolver, as he would certainly have used them if he did. In effort to be friendly, and with a double motive, Bill said, "You're on duty early, ain't you, Mister?"

"It's none o' your business. I'm on early enough to ketch you birds."

Bill walked two feet from the detective, while I was about four feet from him.

"If he has got a gun," I thought, "he's liable to plug me if I run, and that would be worse than a term in jail."

The moon rose higher and the rails shone brighter. A "wildcat" engine came screeching down the yards. It was followed by another engine and flat cars with ropes and other wrecking paraphernalia.

"Been a wreck somewhere?" said Bill.

"Shut your mouth, ye damn parrot. Talk to yare ayquals."

"Ain't you my equal?" blurted out Bill. It was an unfortunate rejoinder. The man did not answer, but gave him a back-handed slap with the blackjack.

Bill started forward but restrained himself. I was glad of his decision, for we were not over sixty miles from the scene of the fight with the other detectives. If we were caught, it meant a term in jail, or the Pontiac Reform School. Bill must have felt the same way about it. It may be that the detective was more fortunate than he knew, as "road-kids" are relentless and vicious in a fight. They have more initiative and energy than older tramps, and they will fight harder for freedom.

We walked along with the detective, whose thoughts kept rambling on an unpleasant subject. "You kids'll git Pontiac. That bunk about sick people don't go wit' the judge. He'll soak ye all. If he don't, I'll quit. Ye guys are the ruin of the country, a bummin' honest people, an' a stealin' money, an' a breakin' into cars, an' a burnin' barns." The detective talked on and on.

A yellow road crossed the tracks. The corn rustled in the fields as the wind blew over it.

"I wonder where the dickens he's takin' us? I thought. And then, "I might as well take a chance." Suddenly there was a wild yell, "Run, guys – run!!!" thundered Bill. He turned swiftly, and gave my arm a quick jerk, and the two of us were suddenly tearing down the road for dear life.

The man stood in the middle of the tracks, and wailed like a man whose professional pride had been hurt.

"Come here, ye little hobo devils," he yelled.

We ran about a hundred yards when Bill said, "Duck over'n the cornfield, Red."

We walked daringly back through the corn toward the tracks at the crossing. No one was there. "The other two guys must of run the other way, and the dick figured he could get them easier," I whispered.

"Them two'll knock hell outta him now, if he tries to catch 'em. They're wise enough to know he ain't got a gun by this time."

"I wonder if he thought we'd walk along to jail with him like little lambs," I laughed.

"He got left if he did. But what was you thinkin' about while you walked along with the dick?" asked Bill.

"Same thing you were, Bill, I guess. I was prayin' for a clear track for a getaway."

"I had a notion to bust him when he hit me with the jack, but I thought I'd better not. I don't wanta make Pontiac again," declared Bill.

"I'd have slammed him before we went to jail. Wouldn't you?" I muttered.

"I'll say I would, and slammed him hard," whispered Bill.

The quick footsteps of a man were heard. Then several dogs barked loud and long. "I wish to thunder they'd stop," sighed Bill.

A man walked from the other direction and stood upon the tracks. He looked about him. We watched him. The dogs stopped barking, and the wind stopped rustling the corn. It became very quiet.

"It's the dick," I whispered.

"Sh-shh-shhh," was Bill's answer between his teeth.

The man stood awhile, then murmured aloud, "Damn their souls," and walked slowly back toward the town.

CHAPTER VIII
BILL'S STORY

CLOUDS FORMED IN THE EAST and bulged upward across the sky. At first they were white and blue dots travelling in regiments of scattered wonder. The largest of them broke as it reached the moon, and trailed a foggish blue and gray mist over it. Then stars and moon seemed to travel rapidly from the clouds, until a great mountain of dark vapour appeared suddenly from the west, and spread like an ocean of ink above the inverted bowl.

An intense darkness covered the earth. Then a tiny white opening appeared in the east, through which one star shone. A swift wind blew across the corn field, and the blades rustled as though an army marched through it. Another wind followed the first one, and whistled along the track like a gale through an empty barn.

The white opening closed and blotted the star from view. The clouds above scattered, then merged together. A roar of thunder shook the earth, and streaks of lightning blazed jaggedly to the horizon.

"We'd better beat it down the track for shelter," I suggested.

"Nope," returned Bill, "we'll cut through the field. I don't like to walk along the tracks in a storm. The steel draws the lightnin'. I seen a bum git struck dead on a track once. It turned him blacker'n a Jew's derby. He jist threw up his hands and fell ker-flop on the ties. It burned his clothes off, too."

We walked through an open place in the field about a hundred yards from the railroad. One gust of wind followed another, and a few large drops of rain fell. Suddenly a streak of light travelled along the fence with ripping speed. "She hit the wire fence," said Bill. "It's a darn good thing we moved from where we were."

As we came to the edge of the cornfield and observed a straw stack standing a few hundred yards away, Bill said, "Let's beat it for there and bore in."

Between flashes of lightning and one thunder clap after another, we ran to the stack and succeeded in making a straw cave before a deluge of rain swept over the field.

We slept soundly.

When morning came, the sky had cleared and rain drops glistened on the wheat stubble under the early risen sun.

A black rooster scratched the ground near a house a short distance away, while several white hens scrambled after the proceeds of his labour.

"I see where we eat," laughed Bill. "Let's go."

As we made our way to the road, we saw a large brick building upon which was a slate roof and many lightning rods. Many smaller brick buildings surrounded the larger one. "Gosh, that looks like Pontiac, but thank the Lord it ain't," murmured Bill, as we walked into the yard in front of the house.

An aged bull dog waddled toward us from near the corner of the house. It grumbled until I stroked its head. This act brought peace at once. We followed the dog around to the kitchen door.

A heavy German woman answered our knock. Without hesitating a second, she opened the door and invited us inside.

Seated at a table in the kitchen was a ponderous man with a bald head, a red beard, and a close-shaven upper lip. He was not to be made uneasy by the entrance of beggars, so he finished drinking the coffee out of his saucer. As the liquid disappeared, his first finger could be seen stretched in the saucer, like a log in a pond from which the water had been drained.

Neither man nor woman was loquacious. When the man did speak, he uttered half inarticulate guttural sounds that seemed to work their way painfully out of his heavy throat.

The ancient bull dog opened the screen door and waddled clumsily across to his master. The man scratched the top of its head with his fingers, while the dog stood as still as a statue. When the man withdrew his hand, the dog looked up pleadingly, and noticing the look, the farmer resumed scratching the head again.

We did most of the talking, and found the people interested listeners.

"What's that place over there?" asked Bill pointing in the direction of the brick buildings.

"The Poor House," answered the woman.

"I thought it might be the Reform School," returned Bill.

"Naw, naw," grunted the farmer.

"You boys ain't from Reform School, be you. No runaways, huh?" asked the woman.

"Nope," replied Bill, "an' I'm darn glad of it."

"Two boys ran 'way 'bout month ago, an' man down the road told police on 'em. He got t'irty dollars for tellin' on 'em, an' dey go back to jail few more years." The woman shook her head slowly. "Men do anyt'ing for money," she continued.

"I'll say they will," commented Bill. "I know a farmer who took a runaway kid in from the Ref. He gave him a nice flop in the best bed, an' the kid was poundin' his ear for dear life, while the farmer was drivin' to town to tell the cops on 'im. That was me."

The farmer and his wife nodded their heads as though entertaining tramps and amateur convicts was a daily occasion.

"Well, Sir, that was funny," chuckled Bill.

"The guy was too darn kind, an' I felt leary someway, an' woke up with a scared feelin', an' put on my rags and sneaked out the front door and climbed up an old apple tree to watch things. I knew I couldn't git far away, so I just took the big chance. It wasn't long before the farmer came drivin' back with two other guys drivin' after him. I could hear 'em talkin' when they popped their heads in the bedroom. They opened the front room door after a bit, an' Mrs. Farmer came out. I could see the light shinin' on 'em all, an I knew the one man was the Sheriff because I'd seen him at Pontiac. He was sore as he said to the farmer, "Why didn't you bring the kid into town with you? We'd have nabbed him there. It's like huntin' a needle 'n a haystack now. Some of them kids are bad actors. He's liable to figure out that you've double-crossed him an' come back here an' burn the house down. You can't never tell.'

"I almost giggled out loud for I could see the guy look scared like a kid caught swipin' candy. 'Which way do you reckon he went?' the farmer asked the Sheriff. 'I don't know,' blabbed out the Sheriff. 'He didn't even let me know he got away from Pontiac. He never told you he wouldn't flop here all night, but he let you drive to town like a boob, and here we all are, like a bunch of damn fools, over a fifteen-year-old kid.'

"Just then an apple fell from the tree and busted the Sheriff on the head. 'What the hell, here! The kid's throwin' apples at us.' I darn near fell out of the tree. Then a darn-fool bird got excited an' started to chatter as though I was coppin' her eggs. I felt like a yegg opening a safe an' findin' a dick sittin' in there wit' a gun pointin' at him. Finally the yap and his old lady went in the house, and the Sheriff and the other guy went in after them. I had a notion to climb down and beat it, and just then they walked out in the yard again. They climbed in the rig and drove away, and the farmer beat it in the house and soon all the lights were out. Somethin' just kept sayin' to me, 'Old boy, you lay low. You might stick your foot in a trap.' I kept quiet, and could hear the bird talkin' to itself in the nest, for birds dream just like people.

"Finally, a guy came walkin' along the road alone. I watched him walk all around the house and barn. You could of sold me for a dime, for I was so scared I darn near shivered myself out of the tree. The man walked back in the front yard again, and stood under the tree for a long time, and I kept worryin' about the bird, but she just talked low to her eggs. The fellow walked down the road, and I was about to climb from the tree and beat it the other way, when I'll be danged if he didn't walk back again.

"Being about all in, I dozed off, and dreamt I was a long ways from the Ref, and the rotten grub, and the snitches, and mean guards. I started to fall and woke up and scared the bird out of her nest, and there was the guy standin' out in the road. I made up my mind that if he left again I'd beat it out of the tree, for if I got caught up there in daylight I'd have to stay all day. He beat it down the road again, and I beat it and run around the house and back of the barn. I lay there behind a big manure pile to get my bearin's. Pretty soon I heard a rig drive in the barnyard and stop, and I dug a hole in the manure pile just like we did in that straw last night. The ammonia darn near choked me. The Sheriff and his deputy stood right near the manure pile, and I could hear him say, 'That kid hain't gone very far, surely. I've got a hunch, he's right around the barn here.'

"'Yeah,' the other man said, 'he's liable to be hotfootin' it ten miles from here by now.'

"'Maybe so. Them little devils are harder to ketch than the old birds,' I heard the Sheriff say.

"I couldn't stand the ammonia in the manure any more, so I fixed a hole big enough to get my face out so's I could breathe. I kept thinkin' what a boob I was to trust that farmer, but then, I thought, 'I was so darn hungry I had to take a chance on somebody, and if they'd of caught me stealin' they'd of soaked me a few years more.' I got dopey, and must of slept a couple of hours. When I woke, I didn't know whether the guys were there or not, but I thought, 'The devil with 'em,' and beat it right across the fields till I came to a haystack where I flopped till about noon the next day. I woke up so hungry my belly thought my throat was cut – so I started to walk again. When I saw a guy a little ways off hoein' corn, I made up my mind I'd give him a chance to git fifteen bucks for turnin' me over to the cops. I beat it over to him.

"I felt tickled when I saw his face, for I could tell he wasn't a farmer, but an old hobo booze-hound. He was jist gettin' over a black eye, and his nose was crooked, an' his little finger was cut off. I could tell he was a bum all right, so I walked right up and told him my story, and how I was hungrier than a tramp in Texas. I kin see the old guy laughin' yet, when he said, 'No – Gawd – you ain't that hungry.'

"The tramp told me he heard everybody talkin' how I had done the farmer out of the fifteen bucks. He said, 'Listen, kid, I'll go in an' eat. They don't lets me eat in the house, but I'm glad of it now. You wait here an I'll bring you a lot of grub an' a can of java. Then you kin beat it back to that haystack an' lay low till night, an' I'll fetch a lot more grub an' java over there when it's dark. I'll have a day's pay comin' an' I'll bum the apple knocker for a buck and give it to you.'

"I flopped in a fence corner till he came back.

"The old guy brought me the grub, and I beat it to the haystack. He gave me three magazines too. Two of them was farmer papers, but I read everything in 'em, how to raise hogs an' chickens an' cows. That night the old boy came again, and gave me the grub an' the buck, an' I beat it about ten o'clock when the hobo went over to flop. I made twenty miles by mornin', but got picked up in Chi, an' they took me back anyhow, but that farmer didn't get the fifteen bucks for givin' me up."

The heavy farmer rose at the end of Bill's story and stood looking out of the window with his hands in his overalls pockets.

"You serve long time?" he finally gulped at Bill.

"Around five years," answered Bill.

I noticed a weary look came into Bill's face as he answered with half-shut eyes. The woman busied herself making sandwiches at this moment.

"Did you learn nothin'?" asked the farmer.

"I learned more how to be a crook than anything else. A lot of things you wouldn't believe if I told you. There wasn't a kind guy in the whole joint. Lots of crooks learn the game in Reform Schools, believe me."

In a few minutes grateful goodbyes were said to the kindhearted couple, and with sandwiches wrapped in paper, we went happily down the road.

CHAPTER IX
A MIX UP

NO BREEZE BLEW ON THE PRAIRIE. Not a cloud was in the sky. Insects droned lazily along the road, and grasshoppers remained in one place long moments at a time. An immense butterfly with brown and white dotted wings flew along the track, and made an attempt to light on me.

"You can tell it's goin' to be a scorcher," I said to Bill. "Nothing has any pep early in the mornin' on a hot day."

We walked for some miles until we came to a freight train on a sidetrack, near a little town. It was not over ten cars in length, and the heavy engine puffed slowly like a tired horse breathing at the end of a long furrow. A few whirls of smoke came from its stack and curled in the air like little lost clouds hurrying back to the sky. The train crew lounged lazily along the track and gave us no sign of greeting.

Some men worked in a yellow field, and the noise of a binder echoed through the still air. It travelled to the far end of the field, and its clicking noise subsided like the last weak strokes of a hammer on a steel rail. The music of a church bell rolled over the fields, and down the track, and on forever into silence.

Suddenly a faint rumbling was heard in the still country, like the rolling echo of thunder in a far off place. It grew more and more distinct, and then a louder and mightier rumbling was heard. The shrieking of an engine whistle split the air, and the ground vibrated. Some quails, startled, flew from a fence corner.

A cloud of dust whirled along the track and the mail train became a faint speck as it thundered toward Chicago.

"She's sure ramblin' hell bent for election," declared Bill. "I wish I was on her. She'll be in Chi in no time."

The freight train moved slowly off the side track. "We can't keep out of sight, as the train's too short and the country's too flat. All we kin do is take a chance on the shacks and con bein' regular guys," said Bill.

In a few moments, we were aboard the train, and in another few moments, we were put off. We stood where a road crossed the tracks, and as the caboose rolled by we put our hands to our noses, while the conductor stood upon the rear platform and shook his fist at us.

We circled through the town, and forgot the train and its hostile crew. "Gee, it seems like a year since last night. I wonder how that dick feels. You notice they ain't hardly any bums travellin' along here. That's always a bad sign. Tough country – they get the word, and steer shy. Of course a lot of them are up in the harvest fields now," mused Bill.

"I think that's where I'll go, Bill. I'll stay a couple of months in North and South Dakota. Why don't you come up with me?"

"Not me, 'Bo. I've got enough hoboin' for this year. Every danged thing goes wrong. I might make a trip or two between Chi and Cincy or Cleveland, but that's all."

We loitered on the streets of the town a short time and returned to the railroad at a slight elevation of perhaps thirty feet. Beyond, the country stretched like an immense checker-board, dotted all over with squares of green and yellow. Not a tree was in sight. The corn stood as still as dead trees in a forest, while waves of heat rolled over it.

A string of box cars stood about a mile below the town on a side track. We looked back at the depot. "I wonder if that's the same freight. Gosh – , I hope not," sighed Bill, as we walked toward it.

"It must be," I replied, "because there ain't a clear track yet. The signal's against them."

As we drew near the train, Bill said, "They ain't much use. You kin see a field mouse in this flat country. They'll be layin' for us, anyhow, but we'll beat it across to that cornfield, an' try an' make it when it pulls out."

Entering the field, we walked toward the train and waited. At last a fast mail thundered through on its way to St. Louis.

Hiding at the edge of the field until the engine and a few cars passed, we made a dash for an open box car and sprang into the door as the train gathered momentum.

Once safely inside, we peeked out of the door in the direction of the caboose. A man's head was seen to pop back from the window. "It's dollars to doughnuts the shack saw us," I wagered.

"Maybe not, Red. Let's hope he's blind. Let's eat this lump, anyhow." We ate the sandwiches which the woman had given us, and then made ourselves more at home by hanging our coats and hats on nails in the car. We closed one door and sat against it while we looked through the open door opposite.

Suddenly the noise of many feet was heard on the roof above. The door was pushed shut at once, while a hammer was heard pounding on the already closed door. We were on our feet instantly.

"They're tryin' to nail us in," yelled Bill, as we rushed to the recently closed door so as to open it before the nails were driven in. We slammed it back with a screeching noise. The men at the top worked at a disadvantage, as they did not dare lean too far over the side for fear of diving suddenly to the ground below if the train lurched.

The man who held the hammer became enraged at the useless effort of trying to nail a door that would not stay still. He threw the hammer viciously in our direction. It struck Bill on the shoulder and fell to the floor. "Pick it up," yelled Bill. I grabbed the hammer and cracked a man's arm that hung below the roof. Feet were heard scampering above as the train stopped suddenly with a violent jerk and threw us to the floor. We scrambled to our feet and jumped out of the door. The entire train crew awaited us outside.

I butted the engineer in his protruding stomach, and he grunted heavily and rolled on the ground. A brakeman pulled a blackjack and missed my head, but the force of the blow threw him forward on the ground. The conductor grabbed at me as I zigzagged the hammer swiftly to right and left. He missed me. Bill threw a grimy fist in his eye. The fallen brakeman had not yet regained his feet, and seemed in no hurry to do so. The fat engineer sat on the ground and thought, perhaps, of a more peaceful scene. In a sudden glance, I saw the conductor's black eye, as he lay with his head on his arm.

The two brakemen and the fireman hesitated a moment, as men will who know not whether to charge or retreat. Bill grabbed the hammer from me, and rushed fiercely at the cowardly brakeman on the ground.

"Gimme that blackjack, or I'll break your jaw in," he yelled. The brakeman handed the blackjack over as though Bill were the conductor of the train. Bill gave me the hammer again.

With hammer and blackjack we rushed at the hesitating three, working the instruments before us as a swordsman wields a sword. The fireman alone blocked our advance, and Bill made a pass at him with the blackjack as though he would drive a spike into his head. The man's eyes opened wide as Bill suddenly shifted and hit him square on the nose. The blood spurted. The man groaned and collapsed.

We rushed to the end of the train, and crossed to the opposite side, and hurried through a cornfield in the direction of the engine. "Let's beat the damned thing out on the rods," snapped Bill. "They'll never think we've got nerve enough to ride the train out now, an' they won't look for us underneath the cars."

Dashing across to the train again, we were soon clinging to the iron rods underneath a car.

The engineer, fireman, and head brakeman walked so close to us on their way toward the engine that we could have reached out and touched their hands.

The engineer was saying, "I don't know what the hell I mixed up in the damned fracas for. I ain't a railroad dick, an' I don't get paid for havin' my guts butted out. That damned kid's part goat."

"Did you see that blond kid battle? Holy jumpin' turnips! I thought he hit me on the nose wit' a sledge," said the fireman.

"The con's goin' to put the cops next when we hit G———, an' they'll come out an' git em."

The voices died away, while we still clung to the iron rods and looked at the rails beneath.

In a few minutes the engine whistle blew two sharp blasts, the signal to leave, and the train was soon on its way. Small stones and gravel blew in our faces, and the wheels clicked monotonously as they rattled over the rails.

The train stopped for some time in G———. At last it clattered over the interlocked tracks of another railroad that crossed there. "I wish I had my coat," I sighed.

"Me, too," replied Bill. We had left them hanging in the box car.

Stiff and sore, we left the train at J——— as dusk fell over the earth.

CHAPTER X
THE ROADS DIVERGE

"IT'S TOO LATE TO BUM ANY GRUB. Supper's over," exclaimed Bill. "How much money you got, Pal?"

"Twenty cents."

"Well, I got a dime. Let's find a saloon that's got a free lunch," suggested Bill.

We found a place a few blocks away from the railroad. A crowd of workingmen stood at the bar, which was lined with large, heavy glasses filled, or partly filled, with beer.

We ordered beer, and helped ourselves to the free lunch without shame. Bill ordered two more glasses of beer with his last dime. If it had not been the law of the road, it would still have been Bill's law – to spend all and break even to the last.

"I got another dime, Bill. We'll go fifty-fifty with it," I said.

"Nope, the devil with it. We'll get two more beers. A guy may as well be broke as have a nickel."

"Better come with me, Bill," I urged.

"Nope, I'll hit the stem and beg enough to get me to Chi on a street car. She's only 'bout thirty miles now."

The two of us walked to the railroad yards where I was to take a freight for Davenport, and from there to the wheat country.

We made a strange appearance. I was hatless and coatless, and my shirt was badly torn across the back. Bill's shoes were held to his feet by small wires. His trousers were torn at the knees, and he was also coatless. But care walked not with us. We had just eaten, and we hummed a hobo ditty.

> "No use to worry 'bout to-morrow,
> For it may never come—,
> For they ain't no use to look for sorrow,
> When you're way out on the bum.

"One time a hobo worried sick
For fear he'd miss a train,
An' it come long an' bumped him slick,
An' rid 'im of his pain."

Thus humming, we reached the far end of the yards and waited for a train for Davenport.

It came at last, and I bade Bill a hasty farewell, and climbed aboard.

"See you in Chi in two months, Bill."

"Sure thing, Kid. Be good. Watch for the bulls at Marion. They used to be hostile."

"All right. So long, Old Scout," I yelled.

The train curled like an immense dark snake before it straightened itself on the main track.

As it rumbled along the rails, the engine whistle shrieking for crossings, I stood on the bumpers between two cars and dreamed of many things.

Now and then a languor came over me and my eyes became heavy. I gripped the iron brake-beam until my wrists ached and tiny particles of rust worked their way into the palms of my hands. The roaring train lashed through the air. The wind blew viciously between the cars. It nearly blew the torn shirt from my body. My hair was wind-tangled and full of cinders.

I had been told on the road that by long practice hoboes could sleep while standing up on the blind baggage of a mail train. I doubted this, as Bill had told me of a man who had been riding the Limited out of Cheyenne with him one bitter night. The man was half drunk, and all Bill's prodding could not keep him awake.

"You better git off the next stop. She's only twenty miles now. You kin never stand the gaff," said Bill.

"All right, Mate. I'll vamoose at the next stop," the man answered, and his bleared eyes half closed as he spoke.

In a short time, the train lurched quickly at a sharp curve, and a shriek went up like that of an animal in pain. Bill grabbed at the falling body of the man, and nearly fell under the train himself. He caught the tail of the man's coat. It ripped up the back, and in another second its owner had disappeared. Bill held a piece of the coat in his hand.

An aching came into my muscles, and my head went dizzy for a moment. It cleared and became lighter. I grew alarmed, but the train rolled on oblivious of a hobo kid with light head and aching muscles.

I wore a heavy leather belt several sizes too large for me. This I unbuckled and fastened around the center of my body and the brake-beam. Breathing easier after this, the fate of the unknown hobo passed from my mind.

A cold sweat came out on my forehead and body. The wind dried it quickly, and I grew chill.

After four or five hours, I reached Rock Island, across the Mississippi river from Davenport, Iowa.

Three cities are at this point of the river, Rock Island, Moline, and Davenport. The mighty river rolls, a sheet of turbid yellow water, a mile wide, between the Illinois and Iowa shores.

Too weary to go far in search of shelter, I slept in a lumber yard on some fresh pine boards until morning. The odour of the wood was not unpleasant, and I soon slumbered like a worn-out soldier at the end of a long day's march.

I was awakened in the morning by workmen moving lumber. A man wearing a carpenter's apron saw me crawl out from under the boards.

"Hello, Kid. On the turf, eh?"

"Sure thing."

"Ain't you got no hat even?"

"No, I haven't, " I answered, as I ran my hands through my hair.

"There's one hanging up in the shed here," said the man. "It ain't much, but it's better'n nothin'."

I walked to the shed with the man, who handed me a white hat which he took from a nail on the wall. I placed it on my head, and it quickly fell to my ears and rested there.

The man laughed at the picture I made. "It's better'n nothin'," he repeated.

"Yep," said I. "Thanks. It's better'n nothin'."

I was soon out of the lumber yard and at the back door of a house on a side street. I had no luck in obtaining food there, and none at the next four houses. The woman at the sixth house invited me into the kitchen and warmed up the remainder of the family breakfast for me.

She wore a tightly fitting calico dress, buttoned down the front. Her face was intensely sharp, and her eyes danced nervously. Her hair had been artificially waved over her ears, and completely hid them from view. She wore a wedding ring that was several sizes too large for her shrivelling finger.

She kept up an endless chatter while she prepared the meal, and I, always reticent with those of whom I begged, was slightly confused. But that concerned the woman not at all. I was a good listener, and she was sorely troubled. "You know," she said, "I never turn anybody away from my door, for I have a brother who is on the road somewhere, if he's alive, and I wouldn't like anyone to turn him away hungry." I felt sorry for the woman, but at the moment I was quite glad that her brother was a tramp. She prepared me a "handout" as I ate at the table.

The woman noticed my torn shirt, and went into another room and returned with one several sizes too large for me. It was a black shirt with white stripes, of a type seldom worn by hoboes. The usual shirt worn by tramps is one made of black satine, and is called a "thousand-mile shirt" for the reason that it can be worn on a trip lasting hundreds of miles, or weeks at a time, if necessity arises.

Thanking her for the shirt and the small package of food, I walked out of the yard thinking of her wandering brother.

Near the river I met another hobo who looked as though he had been in a brawl.

"Which way, 'Bo?" I asked.

"Goin' down to scrub up. Come an' go 'long. I jist bummed a towel and some soap. Woman said her brother's a bum."

"The devil she did. Was she a little skinny woman, gabbier'n a parrot?" I enquired.

"Naw, this jane's bigger'n a sprinklin' wagon," answered the tramp.

"Gosh, they must all have brothers on the bum. A woman told me that this morning, too," said I.

"Zazzo? Well, I bumped into a nice little rumpus over'n Clinton t'other day. Some 'boes fastens a couple o' dicks to some trees wit' their own bracelers. I comes a whistlin' in there like a cattle train. I'd heard o' sappin' days in other states, but I never bumped into one in this 'un before. Well, sir, they ketches four of us and makes us run the ga'ntlet, and believe me, I run. The natives stands on each side for a quarter of a mile or more. It seems like a thousand miles to me. They hit us wit' stones and whips. All them yaps could see was the bottom o' my feet hotfootin' it down between 'em. Some guy caught me wit' a rock here where you see this bump. One o' the bums fell down behin' me, an' they all crowds aroun' him and beats him up good. That give me a chance to get outta some o' the beatin'.

"I'll bet there was two hundred men there, an' a dozen women. I guess a bum deserves a beatin' up, but I didn't do nothin' to them people, an' I didn't even know that anybody beat them dicks up."

The tramp's face was bruised and he grunted as he walked. He carried a ragged coat across his left arm. His sleeves were rolled above his elbows, and his right forearm was black and blue.

I walked with him until we came to a secluded spot at a bend in the yellow water, where we bathed.

The hobo's body was black and blue in spots. His face twitched as he rubbed the soap over it.

After we had bathed and dressed, we sat on the bank and watched a passenger boat ploughing slowly through the water in the direction of New Orleans.

"I went down this river from St. Paul to New Orleans in a canoe four years ago. Had the best time I ever had in my life," said the bum with the bruised body.

"Have you been on the road long?" I asked.

"Dang near all my life," was the reply. "I been darn near ev'rywhere in the world. I druv stakes wit' Barnum's circus all over Europe, Aziah, Aferca, and hell's half acre. I s'pose I'll stay on the road all the rest o' my life, 'less I run into a couple of more sappin' days." There was a silence for some moments, which was followed by the hobo's question, "You been on the road long, Kid?"

"Not so long," I replied.

"Ever have a jocker? You're a purty smart-lookin' boy."

I had long before heard what a "jocker" was in hobo life, a hobo who took a weak boy and made him a sort of slave to beg and run errands and steal for him. I had heard of boys who were called "punks" in hobo life, who were loaned, traded, and even sold to other tramps. The boys who become slaves to "jockers" are of the weaker and more degenerate type. Bill told me of a case where the boy was whipped by his "jocker" for the most trivial offense, and every day of the year he was forced to bring a dollar to him – which he begged.

The tramp always ruled the "punk" by fear. He practiced the same crude and brutal psychology that the pimp practised over the weak woman of the underworld. And always, the boy obeyed with a dog-like affection. Perhaps it was because he had nothing else in life, as, false sentimental reports to the contrary, hobo boys always come from the swollen ranks of poverty and degradation.

I was never able to learn the derivation of the word "punk," as these boys were called, but years later, in more polite society, when I heard it spoken, I experienced a slight shock, as though I were listening to a bishop swearing out loud, or talking intelligently.

I thought of what the one-eyed youthful tramp had said to me so long ago in St. Marys.

"Nope, I'd bust a jocker on the nose that 'ud try to make me out a sucker," I blurted as though I had just happened to think of it.

The hobo looked sideways at me, and winced as he moved his bruised body. "'Course it's all right. Some kids like a 'jocker,'" he stammered after a moment.

"What becomes o' the punk kids when they get big?" I asked.

"Oh, they turn out to be perfessional 'jockers' themselves, an' then they gits kids to be their 'punks,'" was the answer.

My mind turned to Bill and veered to other boys like him. I had heard an old tramp say that once a tramp always a tramp, and I wondered just how many ever left the road for good. I had read of the wanderlust in books, and how it drove men on to far parts of the earth. In spite of all the hardships through which I had recently passed, I found a charm about the road that I had not known elsewhere. I wondered vaguely then about the future, but it soon passed out of my mind, and the immediate problem of the day took its place.

"Is Davenport a good burg to scoff in?" I asked the other hobo.

"Sure thing," replied the sapping-day victum. "There's lots of foreigners over there, and they allus give what they got. Then there's the red light district along the river. Them women'll feed anybody, and they're nuts about tramp kids with red hair. Lots o' times they give cash, too. Do you drink?" asked the tramp.

"Some," I answered, "when I get it."

"Well, get a few snoozers in you an' tell 'em stories and recite poetry to 'em. They fall for that like a yegg does for a safe."

"Yeah, I know. I think I'll hunt 'em up."

I walked slowly along the river with the bruised tramp until we came to the foot-bridge that crossed it. I then left him, and hurried for the water front at Davenport just as the sun reached the highest point in the sky.

CHAPTER XI
A WOMAN AND A MAN

A SQUALID ROW OF HOUSES faced the river in Davenport. No one moved in or out of them. The curtains were completely drawn. A card was inserted in each door, and above the card was a square opening, which was closed by a slide that operated from within.

I stopped at a house which had the title "Madame Lenore LeBrun" on the door. I hesitated a moment, and rang the bell. It clangoured through the house like a bell in a tomb. My knees shook as the slide was pushed back and a voice asked from within, "what you want?"

"Somethin' to eat," I answered.

The door opened, and I walked inside.

A heavy and flabby woman stood under the red light in the hall. She wore a red Mother Hubbard gown. A string of pearls was about her neck, and her left hand was heavy with diamonds. Her eyes were puffed, and deep wrinkles ran from the corners of them. Her hair was artificially blond, and its youthful colour contrasted strangely with her middle-aged and dissolute features.

"So you're broke, huh, Kid?" she said.

"Yes, mum, I'm all out and down."

"Don't mum me, Kid. Call me Lenore."

"All right."

"Nobody up but me. Big night last night. Elks' convention in town. Girls all stewed." And then, "Where you from, Kid?"

"Ohio."

"Damned good place to be from. Only I ain't goin' back. I used to run a joint there on George Street in Cincy. Cops wanted all the dough, so I left."

A decanter, half-filled with brandy was on a highly polished table. Many glasses stood around it, the dregs of liquor still in them. The woman lifted one of the glasses, and noticed the imprint of the bottom of it on the polished table.

"None o' these cats care for a fellow's furniture. Never marry a sport, Kid. They're bum housekeepers. Will you have a shot?"

"Sure thing," I blurted out. My ready answer astonished the woman, and her flabby hand shook as she poured the drink. I tossed it down like a politician. The woman stared incredulously.

"When d'you learn to drink like that?" she asked.

"Never had to learn. It just comes natural."

"Well, it's a bum gift for a bum. Why don't you go to work?"

The brandy teemed in my head. "Why don't you?" was my come-back.

The woman stared. "Well, I'll be damned. The nerve of some people's brats. I belong to the oldest profession in the world. I'm a business woman." Her eyes puckered together. "You're good, Kid. Have another shot. I get a kick out of seein' you drink."

"And I get a kick drinkin'," I replied, as I took the proffered drink and downed it easily. The woman looked intently as before.

"Marvellous. You got a fine drunken future ahead o' you, Kid."

The bell rang again. "That damn thing scares me every time it rings. It sounds like the bell on a lost cow," said the woman. She looked hastily about the room, and up at the gilded-framed pictures of nude women on the walls. I picked up my hat, which lay on a leather lounge.

"Listen, Kid, here's two bucks. Beat it if I open the door."

She pushed back the slide and asked some questions. Men's voices answered.

The door opened, and I walked into the street.

The sun glared fiercely down. There was hardly a ripple on the water of the river. It lay like a great yellow sheet of glasss that had hardened before becoming completely smooth.

The door opened in a house nearby and I heard a player-piano turning out mechanical music. I walked into a restaurant on the corner.

The place reeked of the odour of beefsteak and onions. A waiter took orders with speed and accuracy. "Order of B. and O. (beefsteak and onions). Smother it." A man ordered eggs on toast. "Two on a raft wit' their eyes open," yelled the waiter.

After I had eaten, I walked along the river until I came to a shady spot that afforded a view of the Illinois shore. Two hard maple trees and an elm formed a triangle that sloped toward the water.

As the spot had been used by wanderers before, some paper-covered books and old magazines were in a box under the elm.

I tried to read, but my head was awhirl with a brandied dream.... I would go away to the west and make a fortune. I would come back to the town in Ohio and show the people there a thing or two. I would write a book. I'd go into Chicago and quit the road. To the devil with the harvest fields of South Dakota.... I finally dozed off to sleep and dreamed that I had made a million in Alaska, and that I had returned to devote my time to having a reporter write books which I signed.

Some ants bit me until I awoke and brushed them away. I turned over on my side and went to sleep again.

The sun was half-way down the sky when I awoke the second time. A heavy languor was upon me, and my muscles ached. A cold sweat was upon my forehead. The three trees danced like fantastic green bushes before my eyes. The river compressed itself into a tiny stream and swelled suddenly to a body of water as large as the Forty-Acre Pond near St. Marys.

A tired-looking negro sat under the elm. His shirt was open, and his rimless hat was beside him on the ground. His shoes were near the hat, and one lay on its side. I could see through the sole of it. The man was about forty years old, and very black. His eyes were yellow, large, and soft, with the beaten look of a stray dog's.

I started suddenly when I saw him, for he sat as silent as a black stone on a grave.

"I been watchin' you sleep, white boy, an' you suah slep' soun'."

I held my forehead for a moment, then asked, "How long you been here?"

"'Bout a houh an' a half," was the reply.

"You could of rolled me for my change, couldn't you? I was all in."

"Not me, brotah. I don't roll no one. Dough's hahd enuff to git when you's all in, down an' out. Ah knows."

"Well, listen, I got about a dollar and forty cents. I'll buy the grub and a half-pint of booze if you'll go after it," I bargained.

"That'll be fine. I hain't had nuffin' to eat since mawnin'," replied the negro.

I then hesitated a moment. "Are you sure you'll come back?" and then, not waiting for an answer, I went on, "but I'll take a chance." I handed the negro the money, and he hurriedly put his shoes on and walked gingerly toward the town.

I looked at the river until a languor overtook me, and then, forgetful of the river, the negro, and all, I slept again.

A hand shook my shoulder. The negro, had opened the packages. Crackers and cold meats were spread upon a newspaper on the ground.

"Heah you is, white boy," said the negro.

We ate the lunch in the gathering twilight.

A murky haze spread over the river, and dark and red splotches of colour appeared in the western sky. A gasoline yacht chugged through the water, its lights being visible long after the echo of its noise had subsided.

A quiet gathered around us and, as if in obedience to some deep inner law, we did not talk for some time. Finally, I broke the silence with the usual question of the road, "Which way, 'Bo?"

"Ah's goin' nawth, jist as fah nawth as I kin git," answered the negro. "Ah've only bin outta jail seben month daown saouth. Ah do fifteen yeah, evah since I waz twenty-t'ree yeahs old. Ah pick enuff cotton and build enuff road, an' haul enuff cane to plug up that ol' riber."

"What 'ud they stick you in jail for?" I mumbled.

"I diden do nuffen. Anotheh niggah cuts me wit' a razah, an' I cuts 'im back, an' they soaks me five yeah. The otheh niggah doan even die.

"I serbes my time, an' about the last six months foah it's up, they hiahs me out to some big rich guy daown theah. He kep' me ownin' 'im so much I wuke ten yeahs for nuthin'.

"Ev'ry time I git a paih ova-alls, he charges me some moah, an' tells me I has to wuk it out. I ask him when I git free, an' he say he lynch me ah talk to 'im 'bout that.

"All the niggahs daown in Geoghia gits a dollah if they turns a runway niggah in. Ah know that, but ah takes a chance one time, and floats down the riber on a log. I has a old bull dog, but dey waz nothin' else to do but leabe him. I cried like a little niggah baby on that log, an Ah cries naow when I t'inks ob him. Poor ol' Moses wit' his eah all chawed up a runnin' up an' down the bank a barkin' foh me.

"I floats down the riber 'long time till I meets a niggah an' blabs ma tr'ubles to 'im, an' he wants to tuhn me in foh a dollah. You bet I doan do that no moah, niggah o' no niggah. Nobody t'all. Yu kain't trust niggahs neitha'.

"Ah makes ma way to Memfus, and gits a job, and woaks two month, an' who do Ah see one day but a drummah who sells ma boss stuff in Geoghia. He say, 'Niggah, youh boss evah ketch you, he sure string you up, an' gibe the buzzahds some black meat. You bettah move on.' I was skeered white, an' I moved, too.

"I walks 'way off to Kaintucky, an' I gits a job in Bowlin' Green. I stays theah fouh month, an' the man who I wouk foh laikes me, an' I go to school wit' lotta little kids 'tree mont'. They all laughs 'bout me, great big niggah wit' dem chillun, but ah leahns to read a little. Den who does I meet but dat salesman agin, an' he tries to coax me to git drunk wit' him. Den he tells me he waz offehed two hunder' dollahs to git me back, 'cause I's a good woukin' niggah. I gits skeered and runs 'way from theah an' doan say nuffin' to nobody, nohow. I just keep right on agoin'. Niggah tells me'n Dabenpoaht dat dey kain't takes you back 'less guvanah say so, but I knows bettah, 'cause I knows my old boss. He kills a niggah laike he woul' a snake. I knows – I see 'im do it. Niggah botha him one time, an' he shoot 'im, an' he say, 'Take dat niggah 'way dere,' an' I does. I bet he miss me, 'cause ah use to hitch up hawse an' take 'im church ebery Sunday. I'll say Ah's goin' nawth, an' Ah'll stay nawth, too.'

"You served fifteen years on a five-year's sentence?"

"You bet, an' I ain't goin' back neithah. Dey kin talk 'bout de souf all dey want to, de nawth's good 'nuff foh me."

The colours left the sky. The stars came out. The moon burnished the river into gold.

I looked at the negro, who gazed silently at the water. His face was merged more or less with the night, but his yellowish-white eyes were distinct.

"You've had a devil of a time, haven't you, old boy?" I said.

"I suah has. A niggah ain't got no chance, no time, no wheah, nohow."

"You've heard of Booker T. Washington, haven't you?"

"Yeah, white boy, I's heahd of Jawge and Bookeh both. Dat's 'bout all I knows 'bout 'em. I jist kin read a little in a primah, dat's all."

Late into the night I told the child-like rover about the two Washingtons, and Toussaint L'Ouverture, the negro liberator whom the tricky Napoleon betrayed.

When early morning came, we separated after having coffee and rolls in a dismal restaurant.

I left for Chicago and the negro for Minneapolis.

"I won't forgit you, white boy."

"Nor me you, neither. So long."

CHAPTER XII
A TURN IN THE ROAD

I CLIMBED INTO AN EMPTY GONDOLA that had been used to carry coal, and the black dust was still in it. The trap-doors were open at the bottom, and I could see the road-bed below.

A weariness was on me, and I longed for a quiet harbor away from the jangle and hunger of the road. I wondered where I could get a coat to fit me. The subject of the coat fascinated me, and then my mind became braver, and dreamed of a whole suit.

A gust of wind came along and lifted my hat and carried it straight to the open trap-door. It rolled beneath the train.

Unmindful of the loss, I walked to the end of the car and dozed in the sun.

A rattling and bumping of the cars awoke me at a little town called Bryon. The sun was straight above me, and I decided to leave the train and hunt some dinner.

New switches were being installed along the road. The camp of a grading outfit was a few hundred yards away. Many mules stood about near the camp. Unhitched from the scrapers, they were enjoying the noon-day rest.

I walked straight for the camp and asked for something to eat. A round-shouldered man heard my request and seated me at a table around which the workmen were still gathered.

They stopped talking long enough to greet me, and placed the food near my reach.

The round-shouldered man had a head shaped like a canal boat. He had a long nose, very small ears, and eyes a washed-out blue. His suspender kept slipping off his round shoulder, and he seemed to be occupied half the time in putting it in place with his thumb.

While I was eating he asked, "Would you like to go to work, Kid?"

I thought, of the new coat and answered, "Sure, what'll you gimme a day?"

"A dollar and your board," was the answer.

"All right. I'll take it."

When the noon hour was over, I was taken to a small team of mules that were already harnessed. I drove them to the grade, where a man hitched them to an iron instrument used to carry dirt from one point to another. This instrument was filled at one point and unloaded at another, so that my work consisted in driving the mules ten hours each day. The team could have almost made the trip without a driver, as I often held the lines an hour at a time without speaking to them.

When six o'clock came the first night, I ate a light supper from the tin dishes on the pine table, and dragged myself to bed.

The beds were old mattresses thrown upon the ground. Some of the men had wooden boxes near them. There were none of the ordinary necessities of civilized life. Neither tooth powder nor brush could be seen.

All used the same comb and towel. They washed in basins which were placed on a long wooden bench. As they dipped the water to their faces with cup-shaped hands, they would make loud spluttering noises.

None of the men had home ties, or anything to look forward to when the long grind of labour was over. The men talked of fine women as though they were far-off things, and not of this earth. Like most men, they idealized women too much. I did not learn until years later that both men and women were about the same either at the top or the bottom of society. But those poor devils have probably never learned it.

The fellow is always in demand who can talk about women among men on the ragged edge of life. The poor sentimentalists in the grading camp listened to stories about women told by the round-shouldered man, whose suspender would slip from his shoulder as he talked. They seemed to believe all the stories he told, as they believed the stories of the harlots who robbed them in an hour of the money they had earned by months of tortuous labor.

On the third day, my body ached until I could hardly drag one foot after the other. My forehead was hot as I touched it. The team danced before my eyes as the trees had along the river.

The men were aroused each morning by the beating of a railroad spike upon a piece of iron hung from the branch of a tree near the kitchen.

When it rang the fourth morning, I clambered from my mattress on the ground, and fell dizzily back into it again.

The rest of the men answered the call to breakfast while I remained in bed. The round-shouldered man came in to see me. He looked to be twice as tall, and his shoulders were as broad as his length. My throbbing brain made my eyes flicker and caused the man to dance wildly before me. When he adjusted his suspender, his thumb seemed three feet long, and the suspender resembled the tug on a giant horse's harness.

He said, "Ain't shammin', are you, Kid? You'll be all right by noon," and danced out of the tent.

I dreamed feverishly till noon. I was an Irish general shot to death by the English and dying alone in my camp. I was a poet who recited many verses aloud.

As the trains thundered by, all the hoboes I knew waved wildly at me, and danced, a ragged crowd of madmen on top of the cars. I saw the top of a bridge dash their heads from the train. They still danced, ragged and headless, with immense eyes gazing fixedly from the centres of their breasts.

The round-shouldered man came at noon and at evening. He was convinced that I was not shamming the next day, so he gave me two dollars and told me to go to a doctor. Though scarcely able to stand, I managed to crawl to the man of medicine.

He gave me medicine, and talked of typhoid fever tactfully. I got his meaning. The round-shouldered man gave me another dollar, and I still had fifty cents left. Without bidding anyone good-bye, I boarded a freight for Chicago.

I craved water on top of the hot train. My throat burned and my jaws ached. My head was in a vise, and spikes were being driven through it. I screamed with pain. But the train rattled on through the hot day. My head whirled, and the train seemed to run in a wild circle. I became dizzy, and saw rainbows through which clear water gurgled. I reached for water, and grabbed but empty space.

Determined to leave the train and get a drink, I climbed down the iron ladder, each rung of which was as hot, burning steel.

Only one thing saved me jumping to my death – the train shrieked for a point called Davis Junction and slowed up ever so little. I did not know it then, nor did I stop to consider the speed of the train. I jumped, and rolled on the ground. How long I lay there I do not know. I found a saloon near the track. How – I know not. I thought about a new coat that dripped with water. I drank a large quantity of it in the saloon.

It nauseated me. The day wore on in blistering sun-scorched hours.

Burning with fever, I was thankful when the sun went down and the heat had subsided.

I still dreamed of the new coat, though my feet were on the ground, and my toes showed through the worn-out upper leather.

I knew where Bill lived in Chicago. He would help me get a coat. I would take a fast cattle train and be in there by morning.

How long I waited, I did not know. The boarding of the train, and many of the incidents at this time are still a blurred memory to me. A few stand out, burned into my brain with fever for ever.

I lay flat upon the top of a cattle car. The cattle bellowed and the train roared, while I clung with hot, sweaty hands to the roof of the swaying car.

The train stopped somwhere along the road, and a brakeman walked over it.

"Git off, bum. Don't let me see you on here again."

"All right, brakie," I said, as the man walked on swinging his lantern across the cars. I did not move.

The engine whistle blew twice, and the train rolled swiftly on. I turned giddily upon my back and tried to count the stars. Suddenly a light flashed across me, and I thought it a falling star. A voice said, "Thought I told you to git off this train."

I sat erect at the words. The man leaned down and grasped me roughly by the collar. I stood up under the pressure of the hand, as the man swayed me backward.

"I'm all in, Mister, or I wouldn't ride your damn train. I'm beatin' it for a hospital in Chi."

The brakeman held the lantern full in my face, and looked away. He stopped a moment, then held the light at my face again. "Come with me," he said.

I followed him to the other end of the car. He jerked open a door above the iron manger that held hay for the travelling cattle.

"Jump in here, Kid," he said, "an' I'll wake you when we reach the end of the run. You kin take the mechanics' train into town in the mornin'. It takes the round-house gang home. You won't need a ticket, so just get right on the train."

I stretched out upon the hay in the narrow manger, and crooned with feverish joy. In some spots the cattle had eaten all the hay, and now and then a long horn would prod my fever-stricken body. My throat ached from thirst, and my tongue was as dry as a withered leaf. My lips stuck together, and my eyelids burned as though matches were being contantly lit under them.

Now and then I would sleep fitfully, and the prodding of a horn would arouse me. I dreamed I had a new blue suit, a striped tie, and bright tan shoes. I dreamed about Bill, and the farm in Missouri. Then I thought of the mosquitoes and wondered if they had anything to do with my illness. Someone had told me that they gave people malaria.

I chewed the hay to work the saliva in my mouth that I might alleviate my thirst.

The notion seized me of going back over the train to the caboose and asking for a drink of water. I pushed the door open above me and the swift breeze fanned my burning forehead.

A cattle train is one of the fastest that runs. It sidetracks only for mail and passenger trains, and sometimes not for them.

I clambered up and stood erect on the lurching car. The engine ahead screeched through the night. White and black smoke rolled over the train and scattered in all directions. Hatless and coatless, with the wild wind blowing through my hair, I watched a blur of smoke trailing toward the sky.

There were a dozen cars between me and the caboose. Death would be with me every step I took. I could fall sideways from the car, or make a mis-step and go down between them. Even my turbulently fevered brain figured all the chances.

"I may as well die one way as the other. I gotta have a drink," I decided, as I stumbled across the cars.

The light in the top of the caboose danced like a maiden with water before my eyes. My foot slipped once, and I grabbed the iron wheel of the brake-beam and worked my way to an erect position again.

"Gosh, that was a close call," I thought.

I made the door of the caboose at last. The conductor opened it.

"Mister, I'm dyin' for a drink. Will you gimme one?"

The conductor's eyes went big at the picture I must have made before him. "Sure thing, Kid," he said, as he handed me a tin dipper filled with water. I drank it without taking a breath, and asked for another. "You sure got a hot pipe, Kid," said the conductor.

"I sure have. My boiler's burnin' up," I answered.

Two brakemen stood near, one of whom had befriended me.

As the train lurched, I fell sideways in the conductor's arms. "Lie down here, lad," said the conductor, as he helped me to a bunk in the car. "We'll be at the yards in a jiffy now."

Dawn reached the end of the division the same time the train did. The brakeman walked with me to the workmen's train, and saw me safely aboard. In a short time it was filled with all-night workers anxious to be home.

I left the train at the end of the run at the far edge of Chicago.

The saloons were open, and I walked into one close by and drank a large glass of beer. My stomach revolted, and I hurriedly left the place.

A chill came over me as I walked along the street.

Two teamsters sat drinking liquor out of a pop bottle. Seeing me, they offered me a drink. The liquor burned my throat and made me even sicker than before.

I reached the elevated train somehow. I wanted to find Bill at the Newsboys' Home, which was on the South Side.

People stared at me. I was hatless and coatless. My face was grimed with the dirt of the road.

A finely dressed woman stepped hastily out of my way as another woman gave me a seat near her. She was little and old and shrivelled, and black ear-rings hung from her ears, and the veins ran like swollen blue worms in her hands. By a curious freak of memory, I would know her this day if I met her on a country road.

I left the train at State and Van Buren, and walked dizzily down the steps. I had heard Bill talk of State and Van Buren, and to my fevered brain there came the idea that I might find him there.

Unable to see my friend, and weary and tired, I walked down South State Street until I came to a fifteen-cent lodging house, in front of which decrepit and unwashed loungers stood.

I gave the clerk fifteen cents, and was taken to a small bed in a small room, which had wire stretched across the top.

All the rest of that day and night I lay in the room dreaming wild dreams, and chanting impromptu verses to ease the burning fever in my head.

Something in my own nature, or born of the road, made me suffer alone.

Uppermost in my mind at this time was the finding of Bill, and the Newsboys' Home. I knew that any inmate of the Home would be given a bed in St. Luke's Hospital and the best medical attention in the city.

All through my earlier years, I had heard that any County Hospital was a fearful place for a poor person. Boys at the Orphanage had even told me how doctors and nurses had given the mysterious Black Bottle to sick people. And that was the last ever heard of them. The Black Bottle contained some deadly poison. In the silence of the night, the sick and wasted one was given a spoonful of it, and the bed in the ward was made ready for another patient.

Less than three months before, I had talked to a broken old tramp who was nearly ready to die. When asked why he did not apply at the County Hospital for aid, the old vagrant replied, "I got a chance outside, but they'll croak me sure there. I doan wanta die a suckin' the Black Bottle."

Granted that this may be nearly all superstition, yet its root may be planted in fact. At any rate, nearly all vagrants believe it, and the older ones cite cases in elaborate attempts to prove it.

I feared not death at this time. I did fear the Black Bottle.

I left the room the next day, and groped my way to the end of the building where a faucet was attached above a dirty iron basin. Thirst devoured, I drank freely of the warm water. My stomach revolted again.

Having twenty or thirty cents left, I went down to a cheap saloon that joined the lodging house. With dishevelled hair, and bloodshot, fever-smitten eyes, I blurted out my agony to the bartender.

That man, with coarse, protruding jaw, and heavy hands and shoulders, listened quietly. "Will you get me to the Newsboys' Home, Mister ? I'll make it then. It ain't over a mile from here."

"Hey, Billy," called the bartender to a man leaning against the wall, "got your truck outside?"

"Yeap," answered the man as he slouched to the bar.

"Take this kid to Fourteenth and Wabash, will you? He's sicker'n a hospital."

CHAPTER XIII
A LONG REST

BOYS OF ALL SIZES romped in the cement yard that fronted the Newsboys' Home. Bill was among the number.

He ran hurriedly toward me. The flannel-shirted truckman carried me in his hairy arms.

Bill ran up the stairs to the Matron of the Home, and quickly pleaded for my entrance.

"Jist long enough so's we kin git him in St. Luke's," Bill told her. The kind woman entered my name on the Home Register, and Bill hurried back to me. Other boys had gathered about me.

They carried me up to the dormitory, while the matron telephoned the house doctor.

This man was one of the best-known physicians in Chicago. He came within an hour.

Bill and other boys scrubbed my face and hands, and tried to work a comb through my tangled hair.

Josephine G. Post, the beautiful silver-haired matron, superintended the work. Ever impulsive, and unused to the touch of gentleness, I cried in her arms.

Finally the great doctor came to the white-washed dormitory. He was followed by two internes. He made an examination, and I can still hear him say, "Typhoid – malaria – advanced. Call the ambulance."

An interne hurried to the telephone. The doctor and the internes left, and presently two heavy policemen entered the dormitory with a stretcher. I was placed upon it, and carried to the ambulance below.

One of the policemen grumbled steadily until I was placed in the waiting vehicle. The inmates of the Home stood in a group about the matron as the wagon of the poor clattered over the cobblestones on Wabash Avenue, and turned toward Michigan Boulevard and the Lake.

In a short time, I was bathed, and clad in a clean night-gown, and placed in a white bed near a window which overlooked the blue water of Lake Michigan.

Sick, and at the point of death many times during the next forty-eight days, still, as I look back, even now, they remain the very happiest in my life.

Always, on the road, and in my earlier environment, I had seen too much of the wretched aspects of existence. Women of the finer sort were far off to me, and their gentleness was unknown. A reader of books all my life, and a lover of things beautiful, the doors of my environment had shut out all people who would talk about them to me.

A fluid had gathered on my lungs which seemed to make the abating of the fever impossible for a long time. Three attempts were made to remove it, and the third time was successful.

A German doctor came through the ward, and tapped above my lungs with his finger, and made a mark with a blue pencil on the flesh. That afternoon a hollow needle, to which a tiny hose was attached, drilled its way to the fluid. It ran into a small bottle at the end of the hose. A drop of it turned green on my night-gown.

There were no more relapses after that, and day after dreaming day followed. There were books and magazines in plenty. I roamed over India with Kipling's Kim, and down the roads of England with Hardy's Tess.

A blue-eyed nurse brought me three other books, *The Mayor of Casterbridge, Wuthering Heights,* and *The Story of an African Farm.*

There was no worry about meals or lodging, and the future was a pleasant haze that never cleared. There was never a harsh word spoken in the ward, and doctors, nurses, and internes seldom passed my bed without pausing for a word of greeting.

The boys from the Home made regular visits, and brought fruit each time. The Matron came and lingered over my bed as though I were her own son.

Often now, when the lines of life are drawn taut, I wish for a haven like St. Luke's Hospital.

When it came time for me to leave, the Matron brought me new clothes and shoes. I hated to go, and the last day was one of regret.

The food at the Home, the water, and the rough life and speech of the boys, were things to which I became accustomed only by slow and painful stages again.

I had been cured of typhoid and malaria, but the fever of the wanderlust still burned fiercely in my breast.

CHAPTER XIV
AN ELECTION VICTORY

ELECTION DAY IN CHICAGO was always a boon to the boys at the Home.

As soon as the polls opened, I went with Bill to see a ward heeler on C——— Street. The man gave Bill the address of five polling places in as many different wards. The name of a man stationed at each place was also given.

We first went to an address on S——— Street, in front of which many unkempt men stood. Two better-dressed men with whiskey-lined faces stood near the door. Bill gave one of the men a paper on which his own name was written. The man looked us over and said, as he turned to a small book which he took from his coat pocket, "Let's see, your name is Edward Ryan. You live at the ——— Hotel, W——— Street, and yours," looking at me, "is William Jones. You live at the same address. Go in an' vote. Then come an' see me."

We did as we were told. The clerk made a mumbling sound as he sat with his feet high on a table, and his chair tilted back. The oath sounded something like – Woo-woo-woo-woo-woo, in rapid jumbled, and then slightly more clear and abrupt speech – "So help me God."

The vote cast, we returned to the man at the door, who walked down the street a short distance and gave us three silver dollars each.

We kept this procedure up until we had voted at all five polling places.

At the last place, in a crowded section on West W——— Street, the individual at the door said to me, "Let's see, your name's Abe Goldstein. You live at 422 Halstead Street. Go in an' vote."

"Listen, Mister, what the devil," Bill yelled. "Do you want to get him pinched? How the devil kin he vote with a name like that and the map of Ireland on his face?"

"Well, it's the last name I have on the list. Take it, or leave it. What's a little thing like a name. A cabbage by any other name 'ud take just as long to cook."

"Listen, Red, I look more like a kike 'an you do. Trade names with me," suggested Bill.

This weighty matter settled, neglected future citizens of America, we walked in and voted.

As we left the voting place, we saw a crowd gathered on the sidewalk. Our paymaster was in an argument with another gentleman. "Listen," he was saying, "Ye can't pull that Englan' stuff 'round here, a shoutin' fer the king in front of an American pollin' place. Ye ought to thank God yere in a free country. I'll bust ye in the beezer, that's what I'll do."

A policeman walked up. "What' 'amatter, Patty?" he asked of the offended one.

"Nothin'. This guy gettin' fresh a little. It's all right now."

"Will I give 'im a ride?" asked the policeman.

"No. Let 'im go this time."

When Patty's indignation had cooled, he walked down the street with Bill and me and turned into a saloon. He ordered a drink for all three, and when the bartender had changed a ten-dollar bill, he shoved three dollars each to us.

"Them damn Johnny Bulls gimme a pain in the ear. I wisht we had a war wit' England."

Bill was the world's greatest yesser. "Yes, Sir. So do I," he answered. When we were out on the street again, Bill said, That's all you kin do wit' 'em guys, yes 'em."

"Yes, Sir," I said.

The early afternoon returns registered a heavy Democratic landslide. In a short time a great Victory Ball was held at the Coliseum.

CHAPTER XV
THE VICTORY BALL

THE COLISEUM is a great building on Wabash Avenue. It is said to be modelled after Libby prison of Civil War days.

Through its door had passed many noted political figures, Blaine, McKinley, Roosevelt, Ingersoll, Harrison, and Hanna. It was in the Coliseum that Mr. Bryan made the Cross of Gold speech, being at that time greatly concerned over labour being crucified with a cross of gold and a crown of thorns. The speech made him plenty of gold, but robbed labour of none of its thorns.

The Coliseum was bedecked this night with flags and bunting. The American flag, whose honour had been so gloriously upheld on Election Day, now hung from every conceivable angle.

The subterranean elite of the city arrived in great numbers.

I stood in front of the building as the two leading aldermen of the city arrived.

One of them was a square-jawed little man, whose clothes fit him neatly. The other was a ponderous man, who walked slowly. Both were saloonkeepers.

The little man had been a newsboy on the streets of Chicago. Born in a happier environment, he might easily have made the laws of a nation. He had political acumen and organizing ability of the highest order. He had learned the elementals of life, and had learned them well. All the pages of his life had been dotted with kindnesses. He was human to the core.

A man later entered the United States Senate, whom this little man had staked to a dime's worth of newspapers, when both had sold them together. He was tenacious and wary in a political fight. He played every card to win, and always with the only ethics he knew. He is possibly worth a million dollars to-day. There are those who say that he has given away many millions.

At one time he owned two saloons. One was an orderly, aristocratic little place, where the big political men of the city congregated. Here, the silent little man could usually be found each afternoon.

The inner history of Chicago for the past twenty years was interwoven with the life of this man. For he was the power behind many a temporary throne in the great city by Lake Michigan.

He owned another, and much larger saloon on South Clark Street, at which the floating population of America had gathered for years. It was one of the largest, if not the largest saloon in the world. Large glasses of beer were sold to thirsty vagrants for five cents. The free lunch was always plentiful, and whether a hobo had a five-cent piece or not, he always ate there.

The floor was strewn with sawdust. The place reeked with the odour of filthy clothes and bodies. Broken, wasted derelicts made it their daily headquarters. Wise men carried their beer with them when they walked toward the free-lunch counter, for the watchful eye of the bartender could not always keep it from being hurriedly gulped down by a thirsty vagrant when the owner's back was turned.

The bar was fully a hundred feet long. A yellow-stained looking-glass ran the length of it.

The saloon was often thronged with curious visitors and slumming parties from far and near places.

Vagrants would stream into the city from every direction. They made their headquarters at the cheap hotels in the ward. It was impossible to prove where their homes were, so they gave the names of other floaters who had registered the year before, and had either died or moved on. It made no difference which. Every floater voted for the owner of the saloon. It was impossible to beat him on election day.

Now a crowd gathered about the important little man who walked with the ponderous man. Both men were of Irish descent. They showed their ancestry in the half-choked smiles that lurked at the corners of their mouths.

I stepped up to the little man. "The guy at the door won't let me in – Take me in, won't you –" I pleaded, as I addressed him by his nickname.

The man stopped a moment, and perhaps thought of his own early life on the streets of the city. "Sure, me lad. Go on in." The doorman stepped back, and I hurried past.

As the two aldermen walked through the door, the band played,

"Hail, hail, the gang's all here."

The building was almost full, and a shout went up from the assemblage. Painted women and furtive-eyed men joined in the cheering. Circled all around was a sea of ten thousand faces.

The floor was as smooth as a looking-glass. The band played a waltz, and the dance was on.

Sinuous bodies of young women glided over the floor. They were guided by the hands of pickpockets and pimps, bartenders and ward heelers, and all that gentry whose hearts were soft, but whose way of life was hard.

Many of the young women were no older than high school girls. But their manner betokened women who had seen and remembered much.

Crowds of women from the red-light district were seated in boxes above the dancers. Red lilies they were in a carmine atmosphere, and they enjoyed it immensely. If they were aware of the day when they would be withered stalks, they did not show it. Inarticulate Sapphos, drunk on the wine of life, they enjoyed what many wise men claim is all we have, the present.

The dance ended and the Coliseum suddenly became dark. Then a great artificial electric moon shone from the topmost part of the building.

The band played a moonlight waltz. I was enraptured with the scene. A glint of the moon shone above the box occupied by the little alderman, whose steel grey eyes did not leave the gliding dancers on the floor.

There was a commotion to the rear of me, and a voice was heard saying, "Take your hand out of that. What you tryin' to do, rob a fellow lodge member? You've got a mitt like a elephant."

Quiet came again, the dancing stopped, and the lights went on.

Dozens of burlesque girls who were playing at the different the-atres in the city, ran hurriedly to the centre of the floor. Dressed in many-coloured tights, they began a wild Bacchanalian dance that brought applause from the thousands of onlookers.

Round about the floor they whirled, their sensuous bodies in a frenzy of glorious ribald motion. Blue, red, and white forms, with blond red, and black hair streaming down their backs, they danced with the joy of life in an hour when it was sweet to be alive.

Robes were thrown about the girls when they had stopped danc-ing. They melted into the throng while the hall was prepared for the grand march.

Meanwhile, in the Coliseum Annex, a fat alderman, tipsy with booze, was impersonating a barber.

"Moler's barber college ain't got nothin' on me," he yelled. "Who wants a shampoo." He waved a champagne bottle above him as he yelled. No one answered, but all laughed. Suddenly he spied a boy from the Home, whose hair seemed to fascinate him. He ran heavily after him in an effort to pour the precious liquor on his head. The boy dodged, and man and liquid fell in a wrecked heap on the slippery floor.

A band of negroes in gay silk colours marched upon the floor. A loudly dressed black led them around the hall. Before many years this negro was to be known internationally as a pugilist – Jack Johnson.

There followed the darkies in silks, a composite gathering of negro types made up for the occasion. Some were dressed as cotton pickers, others as levee roustabouts. Old negresses appeared as scrubwomen, young negroes as bell boys – and older ones as Pullman porters. They sang in harmony:

"Some folks say that a niggah won't steal,
But I caught 'leven in my cohnfiel' –
An' one little fellow was screamin' an' yellin'
He stubbed 'is toe on a wateh-melon –"

And then – louder – like a college yell.

"What's his name? Well what do you think –
He's ouh frien' is Hinky Dink."

Then the Grand March began.

The little Irishman walked arm in arm with the ponderous one. The wall of habitual reserve had gone from his face. After them marched wine agents, keepers of bawdy houses, beefy saloon men, gamblers who resembled ministers, and members of local lodges, women in the first and second flushes of youth, the dancing burlesque girls, and the silken-clad and the nondescript gathering of negroes.

Above in a box, a fat man handed liquor to women from the Red-Light District. "I'm waterin' my cattle," he yelled. The women laughed loudly.

Round and round the marchers walked to the tune of spirited band music.

The lights went out again. The electric moon shone. A great flag, larger than an immense rug, rolled downward from the roof of the building. A breeze played upon it from somewhere. It waved gently back and forth while the electric moon shone full upon it.

The band played, and the great crowd joined in song. A few fine voices from the assembled negroes rose above the rest,

"Oh say, can you see, by the dawn's early light, What so proudly we hailed at the twilight's last gleaming."

And then later, in a low vibrating roll of voices,

"Oh say, does that star-spangled banner yet wave O'er the land of the free – and the home of the brave?"

The lights went on, and the speaker of the evening stood on the platform.

He was a lawyer, more polished than the alderman, possibly from long having been used as a tool. He was the graduate of an eastern college, and the son of an old American family. By obeying orders, he had gone far in city politics. He talked fervently about patriotism, and being an Irish-American, he ended by attacking England.

The audience cheered wildly his closing remarks, "The stars in our flag represent the souls of our patriotic dead, the red stripes, the blood of our early martyrs who made this nation that we might enjoy perfect freedom without thralldom of England." And waving his hand majestically in the air, he continued, "And the stripes of that flag represent the pure souls of our women."

After loud applause, the crowd dispersed. Cars waited on the Avenue to carry the mob away. Taxis moved through the throng. In a short time, the Coliseum was deserted.

Chapter XVI
The Road Again

THE WINTER PASSES, and the warm winds of May made me long to wander again. The whistling of a locomotive on a still night had a lure, unexplainable, yet strong, like the light which leads a moth to destruction.

One night, early in the month, I left on the blind baggage of a mail train with a heavy-set Hollander called Dutch Vander.

A faint star twinkled at the upper tip of a young moon. In the afterglow of sunset, the great Lake, rolling smoothly, loomed, an inland sea, in enchanting mysterious purple.

We waited an hour for the train on a bridge under which it ran. The young moon, still on fire from the sun, dipped a red sickle into the lake. The water purred and broke lazily white on the shore. Then the moon sank into the lake, and the white breakers merged into purple, then the purple into a dark, deep blue. Then the stars shone like diamonds on a huge inverted ceiling.

"It's a peach of a night," said the Dutch boy. And I, with a dream tapping at my brain, replied, "It sure is, Dutch."

The Big Four mail left the Illinois Central each night around eight o'clock. The bridge on which we stood was about nine blocks from the station. To avoid railroad bulls, our plan was to drop from the bridge onto the tender of the engine as it rolled underneath.

As the smoke from the train scattered over the lake, and the head-light of the engine gleamed across the tracks, we climbed over the railing of the bridge. It was a nervous moment. The train drew nearer in a cloud of smoke. At last the engine was under the bridge, and the downward-driven smoke curled in heavy masses in an effort to escape into the air. The whistle shrieked twice, and the train rolled faster. Releasing ourselves from the railing, we dropped safely on the tender. In a few moments, our composure regained, we climbed down and stood upon the blind baggage in order to escape the wind from the lake and the cinders from the engine.

Cincinnati was three hundred miles away. It was our intention to arrive there at eight the next morning. It was considered nothing unusual for "road-kids" to make such a journey in a night. There were many who had made trips from Kansas City and Omaha under the friendly shield of darkness most of the way. These cities were between four and five hundred miles from Chicago.

At Kankakee, Lafayette, and Indianapolis, we were forced to leave the engine and seek a hiding place near the track, but we reached the Ohio city on schedule.

In this city, I had spent six years in an orphanage. When a boy leaves an American orphanage, he leaves it forever. I have never been able to become sentimental over a home for beggar orphans, though coming of a race of sentimentalists who chatter nonsense to God when their very lives are in ruin.

"Well," said Dutch, "we'll have to shake our feet for breakfast." Weary from the long ride, and dirty with the dust and grime of the road, the begging of the morning meal was not a pleasant prospect.

We entered a saloon on the levee near the Ohio river. The bartender showed us the washroom, and gave us a piece of yellow soap and a frayed white and black towel.

Refreshed from the use of soap and water, my courage returned. "Let's beat it for Fountain Square, Dutch, and hit the stem for enough money to buy a real meal."

"I'm on," said Dutch who had the great redeeming features of stolidity, quick decision, and an absence of fear.

During all my years at the orphanage, the fear of the reform school had been drilled into me by the religious women in charge.

The bartender heard us debating the question of breakfast. "I ain't got a dime, or I'd stake you kids, and I can't tap the till. The boss knows how much dough he's got. But I kin stake you to a shot."

"That'll be fine," I replied, as Dutch and I walked toward the bar. The bartender lifted a rusty, stained bottle from behind the bar. The bartender lifted a rusty, stained bottle from behind the bar. He set two small glasses near the bottle, and filled them with the red liquor. It poured as flat and beadless as water. All three of us looked at it, and knowing that good whiskey always had bubbled beads at the top of the glass after being poured, the bartender said with a crooked smile, "It ain't Catholic liquor, kids. It ain't got a bead on it, but two shots o' that and you'll lick the Pope's uncle." We swallowed one glassful and then another. It burned down our throats. The reform school and the fears of my childhood were things that existed no longer. My brain teemed with a mad purpose. I'd get a meal of ham and eggs, or I'd go to jail trying.

Dutch rubbed his cone-shaped head. I laughed outright, "That stuff 'ud jolt a bum off a train, eh, Dutch?"

"I'll say so," replied Dutch. "She'd jolt a train off the track."

We took our positions on each side of the Square, after making plans for a meeting in an hour.

I was lucky at once. A negro labourer in a plaster-covered suit of overalls came humming loudly along the street. I put on my saddest expression, and told him a tale of woe. He grinned, wordless, while I talked. A thousand Irish tellers of tales awoke in me. The negro's yellow-white eyes became misty as I pounded at his heart with words…. I had helped a negro escape a lynching – and I was fired from my job for so doing. I described the black man running down the street with the madder whites after him with a rope. I described how I jerked him into a hallway in a last wild effort of daring, while the crowd rushed on thinking he had turned a corner…. The negro rubbed his eyes, while I talked on and on. Two policemen passed, and for their benefit I changed suddenly to a long conversation about work. Suddenly I got a whiff of the negro's breath, and it dawned upon me that black fairies danced whirligigs in his brain. Weary of the word bombardment, he said, "Let's eat." As is the way of humans, I forgot my companion in misery and walked away with the gentleman in the plaster-spotted overalls.

There was a cheap saloon down Fifth Street way where the races of the earth commingled. We walked inside and sat at the table, each of us now talking at the same time. A heavy waiter ambled clumsily toward us. The negro gave an order for drinks of liquor, while I pounded the table and said, "Bring me food." The waiter looked toward the bar. "Bring 'um food then," said the negro. The drinks came first, and were quickly swallowed. Two more drinks were ordered.

I became tired of talking, my object gained. The negro went on –
"Boss, he say to me, 'Hey Niggah,' an' I say, 'Who you callin' Niggah?
Wheh you t'inks you is, down souf? I done quit.' I frew that 'ere hod
right in the plasteh, I did, and mosies down the street. No guy kin call
me niggah, 'cause I ain't."

"Sure you ain't," I answered, "you're as good as white people any
day. God made us all, an' he knew what he was doin' even if he was a
little colour blind. Do you believe in God?" I asked.

"Does I believe in 'im? I know 'im. God's come to me an' talked
lots o' times. God ain't white. He's blacker'n me. I seen 'im, I did.
Now way long time ago all de people was black, den de sun shone hot
an' all de sick people tuhned white. Then they gits to thinkin' white's
de best coloh, an' gits swell-headed. They can't call me Niggah. I
knows what I's talkin 'bout."

The waiter appeared with a mess of food called "slumgullion" on
a yellow plate. The negro looked at the steaming hot stuff, and said,
"Bring me some o'dat, waiteh." The waiter looked at his darker brother and went away to comply with the order. When he returned with
the food, the negro said, "Bring us some moh drinks."

The negro resumed his talk. "Two hunerd yeahs from now, they
won't be but one niggah lef', and he'll be crippled up. Den all de'll be's
a white man, a niggah, an' a poodle dog. The white man'll kill the niggah, an' use 'im foh black peppah when be eats de poodle dog, an'
that'll be de end o' the niggah."

"Well," I said, "that won't matter."

"Suah nuff it won't matteh to de niggah, 'cause de niggah has a
mohtal soul."

The negro tasted the food, and immediately his mind became
busy with material things.

He ordered another round of drinks. The rotgut liquor made the
black fairies dance wildly in his brain. He swallowed his glassful, and
ordered another one. I reneged.

I shoved the half-eaten food away from me, and watched my
negro benefactor across the greasy, unvarnished table. With tipsy
brain, I tried to figure out the mystery of the races. They marched
before my eyes for a million years back, the blonds and the blacks, the

reds and the yellows. The man in front of me felt that his God was black. The women who had pounded a mock religion into me felt that their God was white, while as a child I had dreamed of Him as an immense man a hundred feet tall, with long red whiskers. And, possibly from hearing other little children cry themselves to sleep, I gathered the idea that He was a cruel man from whom orphans scampered away as soon as their mothers died. In that fly-reeking and dirt-covered saloon my tipsy brain reveled in a tipsy dream. Never will I forget it.

... Countless numbers of girls of all colours, as naked as slender trees in winter, danced on an immense level and yellow stretch of sand, near a blue-green ocean under the light of the moon. Red, white, blue, and green angels flew above them scattering flowers. Their bodies danced in rhythm to the waves of the sea. In a short time the sand was covered with many-coloured flowers, and still the flying angels dropped more. All of a sudden a horn of sand formed that reached to the moon. It circled round and round, as it was blown by the wind. Then millions of varied and brightly coloured birds and butterflies came as if from nowhere. Each bird and butterfly picked a flower from where the sand had once lain, and each flower picked was of a different colour from the bird or butterfly that picked it. Carrying the flowers, the winged beauties flew in circles with the sand that reached up to the moon, which now danced madly in the sky. Then the angels flew after the birds and butterflies. The millions of girls suddenly mounted into the air with wingless bodies and vari-coloured streaming hair, singing the while, a weird, sad song, like a billion Jenny Linds singing together. The stars dropped downward from the sky, and the sun tore a great jagged hole through it in the east. Only the moon remained dancing, a mad fantastic orb of brilliant light above. It circled around in the sky, the very opposite of the circling sand and girls and butterflies. Then the sun came swiftly forward from the east, travelling faster than light. It rolled over the blue-green ocean and dried it up suddenly, as a hot flame dries a drop of rain. Fishes, sea-animals, and grotesque reptiles died slimy deaths in the kelp and coral of the ocean bed. Great whales lashed their dying tails and splashed mud for hundreds of feet, and then lay still. Each little fish and animal attacked a larger one and died a second later. A great wind followed the sun, and swept the ocean bed clear of life, and sent all forms of it whirling, dead, among the flying angels, girls, and flowers. Everything moved with exact precision, and stars and sun and whales and even the tiniest bird carrying a flower, were in no more danger of striking each other than the planets, which had swung aloft in the now empty sky. A girl flew out of the confusing welter of confusion with some ham and eggs on a tray. I reached out for her. A hand grasped my shoulder. "Wake up, Kid. This ain't a lodgin' house." The waiter stood near me, while across the table, the negro, rubbed his eyes.

As we left the saloon, I said to the negro "Loan me a dollar till I see you agin?" The negro laughed.

"Ah'll loan you the buck, but I done won't see you no moah." He handed me the dollar and I hurried away to find Dutch.

The negro was right. He never saw me again.

CHAPTER XVII
A SAMARITAN'S FATE

I HURRIED TO THE APPOINTED PLACE, but Dutch was nowhere to be seen. An hour passed, and still my companion did not appear. The separation of rovers is a common occurrence in tramp life, and at times, owing to the uncertainty of circumstance, the most expert of drifters find it impossible to travel together. Perhaps Dutch had been picked up by the police. Well, he knew which train we had decided to beat to the east. He might show up there.

Hours passed, during which I loitered in Fountain Square, while the sun slid westward in the sky. At last, I made my way to the Kentucky side of the yellow Ohio, and waited for the Fast Flyer Virginia, which was scheduled to leave at seven.

Night stole softly over the Kentucky hills. A large white boat, the lights from its windows shining across the water, worked its way slowly in the direction of New Orleans. Some negroes lolled on boxes in the steerage and chanted an indistinct song, inarticulate dark poets, weary with the labour of the world, sailing back to rest on their wonderful river of dreams. With well-modulated voices, their words glided over the water in a weird and beautiful cadence. Forgetful of the fascinating road of the young hobo, I gave myself up to listening to unknown minstrels, singing to relieve their snarled and wretched lives,

"Oh, my pooh Nellie Gray, they ah taken you away, –
An' Ah'll nevah see mu darlin' any moah, any moah –
They ah taken you to Georgia for to weah you life away –
An' you gone from the old Kaintucky shoah."

The boat glided onward, and the voices became more indistinct. They at last died away, softly, like a June breeze swaying shamrocks over far-off Irish graves.

As the lights of the boat faded, the great headlight of the Fast Flyer Virginia swept over the rails. Aroused from the lethargy of dream, I was the rider to far places again, and my great iron horse was snorting on its way.

I turned my coat collar up, hurriedly adjusted my cap low on my head, and waited with heart pounding nervously as the train approached. It was my ambition to reach Washington, over five hundred miles away, on the Fast Flyer Virginia by the middle of the next afternoon.

Like many ambitions, it was rather worthless itself, but perhaps the grueling grind of the road, the lashing of the wind, the rain, and cinders combined with the smoke and gaseous grime of tunnels, gave me the courage to endure the keener mental tests that met me at the yearly stations ahead, when I learned to write without knowing the simplest rules of punctuation. Indeed, the endurance learned on the road abided with me on many a sixteen-hour day during which I fumbled at a typewriter with the knuckle-cracked hands of the hobo and pugilist.

Years later, when my first book was published, a famous writer, with elaborate condescension, said that it was hard for an ex-hobo to learn to write. I put away the thought with a grim smile, for self pity is one of the things a young hobo learns to discard sooner than do other men who paddle in the softer waters of life.

The Fast Flyer Virginia was rolling swiftly eastward. I dashed for the smoke-enveloped blind baggage, and was quickly aboard. Another vagrant clambered up behind me. He had come from some hiding-place near the tracks. The engine swerved; the whistle shrieked; the smoke cleared away. The face of my companion was visible under the stars. It was Dutch.

"Where the devil you been?" I asked. "I thought you were pinched."

"Not me, old scout. I run into a streak of luck. Met a drunk. Went down to the Silver Moon, an' got a lot of drinks an' a big feed from him. Then I took him in the alley, an' busted 'im in the jaw, an' rolled 'im. He diden have nothin' on 'im though – thirty cents."

"What kind of a guy was he, Dutch?"

"Some shine, blacker'n coal, wit' a pair o' overalls covered wit' plaster."

"It's a funny world, Dutch. The good guys always get it in the neck."

"Damn 'f they don't," replied Dutch.

"That same nigger fed me, I said, "an' gave me a silver dollar."

"The hell," said Dutch. "That's funny."

I wondered how the next beggar would fare who told the plaster-covered darky a tale of woe. Perhaps as well as I did, for a kind heart is a sad heritage of which all the ills of life do not rob a person.

For a long time, as the train whirled through emerald-green Kentucky, I thought of the negro knocked out in an alley for being kind to strangers. And then I thought of the thirty cents of which Dutch had robbed him. I recalled a terrible picture of Judas holding out his hand for thirty pieces of silver. But strangely enough, I did not condemn Dutch, nor connect him with Judas. The ethics of the road are brutal and strange.

CHAPTER XVIII
A WORLD'S RECORD

WE CLUNG TO THE FAST FLYER VIRGINIA for twenty-one hours, climbing the Blue Ridge Mountains, roaring through tunnels, dashing by country stations. We watched the sun rise to the meridian, and then watched it slant westward down the sky. We wished food and drink, but flying trains stop not while hoboes dine. There was only one alternative if we wished to reach Washington, and that was to stand the gaff and stick with the train. It was not easy riding either. We hid behind box cars, or piles of railroad ties at division points. At Clifton Forge, Virginia, we crawled under the engine to escape the eyes of the fireman while he filled the tank with water. We were challenging the combined forces of the Chesapeake and Ohio Railroad, and it was only by being alert and indefatigable that we could win. Passengers waiting for trains at depots would gaze in open-eyed astonishment at us as we flew past the stations gripping the iron ladders.

A test of endurance is a wonderful thing when the blood flows swiftly and the years are young. Twenty-one hours of punishment to satisfy the ego of youthful tramps. There was no object, save that around camp-fires by running brooks we could brag to grizzled and decrepit hoboes how we had ridden a mail train nearly six hundred miles through a populated section of the country. We knew that less daring men in a ragged profession would admire us for the feat. No object at all – yet it was about the same object that actuates the rest of humanity of every class and creed, the admiration that humans have for others who do the thing of which they are not capable, or daring, or foolish enough to do.

With parching throats and smoke-streaked faces we reached Alexandria, Virginia, in the middle of the next afternoon. Leaving the train there, for reasons of safety, we caught a slow freight, commonly called a "drag," across the Potomac river to the edge of the Capitol City.

The Federal soldiers who ran into the city from Bull Run were no whit wearier than we. We left the freight and straggled to a cheap restaurant where we were allowed to wash our sun-scorched faces with cold water.

There was relief in sight. The negro's silver dollar would purchase food anyhow. We walked to the lunch counter and seated ourselves upon high stools. I felt in my pocket for the silver piece. It was gone.

There followed a mortified silence. "I lost the buck, Dutch. Have you got any kale?" I asked.

"Sure, Red. I got thirty cents." He laid the three dimes on the pine counter.

Like men who had dined well, we strolled out to view the city. We walked from the White House down Pennsylvania Avenue to the Capitol steps.

At last, worn out from futile wandering, we spied a box car on a side track. It contained hay. Oblivious of everything but rest, we crawled inside and slept soundly – for a short while.

We were awakened by a man who held a flashlight in his hand. "Pile out o' here," he said.

We crawled out of the car, holding our shoes in our hands. Two policemen stood at the door awaiting us. The man followed us, still holding the flashlight.

"Ah ha!" said the larger of the policemen, "two disperate characters, eh?"

Immediately I framed a tale of a lonely mother waiting for me in a far-off city. Dutch had no home and stayed with me. Work was slack in our city, and we were bound for Baltimore to heat rivets. I ignored the man with the flashlight and the other policeman, concentrating all my attention on the man who had spoken with a slight Irish brogue.

"How old are ye?" asked the man when I stopped for breath.

"Fifteen," I answered.

"Well, well, indade. I have a lad yere age, an' I'd hate to see him driftin' 'round the country like a lost sparrow." The three men started walking with us to a well-lit part of the city. They debated among themselves the advisability of locking us up or turning us loose. It dawned upon me that the man in citizen's clothes was a railroad detective. The police seemed willing to let us go, but were loath to take the initiative, in fear of the detective informing on them. Under the sputtering light of the street, I again probed the well of sentiment in the Irish policeman's heart. He wavered a short moment, and then came to a quick decision. "Ye kin go on to Baltimore, lad, for all o' me," he said. So saying, he walked away, followed by his comrade. The detective followed.

They walked about twenty feet away, when the Irishman turned and said, "Git back to yere flop in the car. We're all willin'."

We turned at once in the direction of the car. "I don't like the look in the railroad dick's eyes," said Dutch.

"Oh, that's all right," I replied. "He won't bother us no more tonight."

We trudged wearily to the car, and were soon forgetful of the road.

We slept, we knew not how long, when we were awakened by a man with a flashlight in one hand and a blue-steel revolver in the other. He handcuffed us quickly and marched us to the city jail.

Our simple belongings were left with the desk sergeant. They consisted of a knife, a comb, and the stray things that find their way to a boy's pockets. We were then taken by a policeman to a large room which contained many cells. The doors of our cells clamped shut with a heavy bang. The policeman sprung a lock on each cell and went shuffling down the dimly lit corridor. The sound of his feet died away, and we were left with our own thoughts until morning.

I sat on the edge of my iron cot and watched Dutch remove his coat and roll it up for a pillow, going nonchalantly about the task of preparing for bed. "I hope to thunder they let me get my sleep out this time," he said.

"They will," I replied.

"Know what?" he asked. "That dick called his pardner. They framed on us just as sure as all detectives go to hell."

"Don't be too sure, Dutch. Maybe it was the Irish cop. All the Irish doublecross each other," I answered sleepily.

"Oh, well, let's flop. They may not hang us," said Dutch.

I stretched out on the iron cot and watched the stars peek through the bars of the window, and wondered what the next day would bring.

The heavy breathing of prisoners could be heard all around me. A bed creaked as its occupant rolled over. In a short time, Dutch slept, his conscience unbothered by the memory of a battered negro in an alley.

Dawn crept through the barred windows of the smudgy prison, and was greeted lustily by the inmates in their cells. A prisoner called out the number of remaining days he had to serve. "Five more days to-morrow." "One moah yeah to-morreh," yelled a negro's voice. This was kept up until each prisoner had announced the remaining days of his sentence.

CHAPTER XIX
THE KANGAROO COURT

THE CELLS WERE UNLOCKED at seven o'clock. We were marched, with other prisoners, to a long table at the end of the jail, where a breakfast of wieners, rye bread, and weak coffee was served. A man with an immense stomach and three chins stood near the table "in order to keep order," as he said.

It was Sunday morning, and, perhaps out of courtesy to President Roosevelt, who believed in the strenuous life, the cell doors were left open so that the derelicts might exchange social gossip.

The prisoners noticed Dutch and myself, and immediately formed a kangaroo court after the meal.

We were charged with breaking into the prison without the consent of the inmates.

A one-legged hobo bailiff led us before "His Honour," a decrepit, bewhiskered derelict who scratched himself constantly. He wore a black and white striped "hickory" shirt, and his right cheek was swollen with a large quid of tobacco. Every now and then he aimed with accurate precision at a square wooden box filled with sawdust. "His Honour" wiped his lips as the saliva spattered into the box, and then his Adam's apple was seen to work up and down like a frog crawling under a yellow sheet.

As we faced the judge, he asked us from which state we hailed. Upon answering "Ohio," a vagrant from that state was appointed to defend us.

The vagrant lawyer from Ohio walked toward the judge and said, "Damn your honour." The one-legged bailiff pounded the floor with his crutch and yelled, "Hear ye! Hear ye! Damn it – can't you hear me."

The fat man who watched us "in order to keep order" was laughing heartily. His three chins and belly shook with mirth.

I had heard of kangaroo courts, and knew that the man who told the wildest tale of a crooked life would find mercy from the court. Innocence alone was frowned upon.

I stood before "His Honour." "Give some account of your life outside, so that we may judge of your fitness to be among us. Speak candidly, an' remember that the court has no mercy on poor men." He spat again, and his Adam's apple worked convulsively. He missed the box. The one-legged bailiff stood near it, and the brown stream ran down his crutch like sap down a maple tree.

"What the hell, yer honour," he shouted, as the crowded court laughed.

"Order in the court," yelled the judge.

"Well, to presume," went on "His Honour," "you are charged wit' bein'a Jesus-shouter when little kids're hungry."

My lawyer answered, "That's a lie, Your Honour. His record's clean as a nigger in a coal mine. He's not an honest man. He denies it. He makes tame girls wild. He runs a Law School. His brother's a perfessor. He's no preacher. While it can't be said he's fool enough to work for a livin' – still, Yer Honour, his hands ain't smooth from pattin' women on the back. They hain't fer a fact."

The prosecuting attorney cut in. His shirt was open at the throat, and a mass of hair covered the front buttons. There was a red birth mark on his right cheek, and a scar at the edge of his temple. He was immensely broad, and immensely short. The bottom of a trouser leg had been torn off, as if by a dog, and the other one was too long and was rolled several times above his shoe, which was cracked across the top. His hands were brown, and when he closed them, they resembled mallets fastened to hairy arms.

"By Gawd, Dishonour, I don't stand for this," he said. "This amb'lance chaser's tryin' to make this kid out a saint. The kid's a sissy. He goes to Sunday School ev'ry Sunday."

The attorney from Ohio answered, "Yer Honour, that's so ontruthful it's disevident to all. The kid's a punk, a Prusshun. Why he's slept in box cars with Frisco Slim. Why he's known as Cincy Red. They ain't no Sunday School boys sleepin' roun' Frisco Slim, is they, Yer Honour?"

"How the hell do I know," returned "His Honour," as he started to spit and changed his mind. "Ask me 'nother question like that an' I'll have you put up for attempt at court. Yere too intimate. I don't sleep with strange hoboes." The prosecuting attorney scratched himself.

"Hear ye! Hear ye!" roared the judge, "Bailiff, this man's scratchin' hisself afore the court. That's a rank disrespect of my judicial perolatives. I order that the attorney be fined at once."

"How much is the fine, Your Honour?" asked the bailiff.

"A dime and his pocket comb," answered the judge.

The bailiff collected the fine and moved toward the judge, who took the dime, saying, "This'll be for the court's expenses. Boil the comb 'n lye an' hang it out in the air six days. Lice won't live on a p'liceman. Give it to the desk sargeant."

The two lawyers proceeded to argue with much bitterness. When they had finished, the judge called me closer to him and said, "My boy, I don't b'lieve none o' the charges agin yu. Ye look like a blowed-in-the-glass stiff to me. I think ye'd eat tramps' leavin's, I do. Ye look as rough as a jungle buzzard. I want to say to you that ye must keep on the way yere goin'. Git sluffed up all ye kin an' in a couple o' years ye'll be an all aroun' tramp.

"Now don't listen to none o' them guys what tells you dif'rent, 'cause you'll fool aroun' and not amount to nothin'. O' course there's some things you could learn and still be a good hobo an' yegg, but then they's allus the danger yu'll go to ruin. You might be an undertaker in a poor neborhood – you might even speak on the Chautaquay platform, or join the Army, or be a admiral's punk in the Navy, or the Chaplain's, but then, yere in danger, and yere too smart fer that.

"We have decided not to try you on the charge o' breakin' into this jail, 'cause in all inhumanity we don't think that even a sentor or congerssman could be dumb enough to do that, not if they lives in this town long enough to know.

"I feels like it's my bounden duty to tell you these things. Yere young, an' the world is behind you, gittin' ready to kick you good. Now the thing to do is sit down all you kin an' harden yourself in weak places so's the kicks won't hurt. That's the way all them business guys do. They gits tired o' furnishin' work for guys to do, so's they calls, 'emselves 'tired business men'.

"I thinks you got a chance to be a good bum, 'cause from your looks it's plain to me that if you had less brains we would sell you to the Zoo in New York. Barnum was right when he said that some o' the people come from apes, Kid. You still got to go through the evolutin' stage before you'll be a ape. Apes is smart, lots smarter'n police or demercats.

"I won't give you a rough sentence, lad. I'll be kind to you. I'll be your Oscar Wilde an' say purty things to you. We'll go out a galavantin' wit the club girls, but I'll be true to you, an' so," the judge looked about the room, and resumed, "the sentence o' this court'll be a light one. All you has to do while yure retirin' from the world is to take care o' the judge's chambers, clean out my cell each mornin', and make the bed whereon I slumber."

Dutch was then brought before the judge.

The bailiff pounded his crutch for order, while the opposing lawyers stood on each side of him. "Yur Honour," began the lawyer for the defence, "I bring before this bar a noted stool-pigeon – a man who tells lies to the screws (police) upon his fellows in the same line of work."

"He's not a stool-pigeon, yelled the prosecutor. "He's an honest hod-carrier. Look at them shoulders, an' look at 'is head – you cou'd shoot it out of a gun."

"His Honour" looked in a puzzled manner at the attorney for the defence. "I wish to warn you aginst looseful use o' language in the future. This is not a bar at all, but a court room where we dispense wit' justice, like ev'ry other court in our broad home o' the free and land o' the slave. This place has none o' the appertainments of a bar. If it had, you wouldn't be lawyerin', an' I wouldn't be judgin' people who hain't been as careful as me."

Dutch stood with folded hands befor the judge, and laughed. "His Honour" frowned from his perch against the wall. Importance descended upon him. He looked as dignified as a tailor Shriner in the regalia of his lodge. "What is the charge agin this young man?" he asked.

"Stool-pigeon, Your Honour," said the bailiff, "an' breakin' in here."

"I believe it. He's guilty of both charges," said the judge. "I fine him all he's got, and sentence him to sweep the jail out every mornin'."

The bailiff searched Dutch. "He hain' got nothin' on him, Your Honour."

"Where is your stuff ?" asked the judge.

"With the desk sargent," answered Dutch.

"Oh, hell, we'll never git it, then," said "His Honour." "You kin sweep the jail out twice a day."

The bailiff swung sideways with his crutch and disappeared. He returned in a moment and handed Dutch a broom, its straws black from many sweepings. Dutch started sweeping violently where he stood. The dust raised in a cloud under the delicate nostrils of the judge, and he coughed. The prosecuting attorney led Dutch to the far end of the aisle, where he began industriously carrying out his sentence. "His Honour" yelled, "Hey, you, cut that sweepin' till the court takes its mornin' airin'."

"The court's dismissed, but detained," shouted the bailiff. The court-room loungers, laughing, formed in disheveled groups in the aisles of the cells, and talked of freights, and crooks, and painted women whom they had known in the days, when life was free.

CHAPTER XX
A WILD RIDE

CHARGED WITH VAGRANCY, we faced the real judge Monday morning. The man who had arrested us was there to tell the nature of our offense.

It had been prearranged that I was to talk in court if the judge should ask questions.

The judge rubbed his face with his left hand, and then looked about the room with the bored expression judges often have who spend years sitting in judgment on the shoddy, the petty, the cast-offs, and the broken misfits of life.

We were not paid the honour of being tried alone. There were at least three dozen other culprits in the room. They sat huddled together, some defiant, some scared, and others as bored as the judge.

A dope-fiend jerked and squirmed on the bench near me. "They won't send me up," he said, in a loud whisper. " My dad's Secretary o' War. He'd turn a battleship on this town if they sent me over." A gavel hit wood – a voice yelled, "Order," and the dope-fiend became quiet, his mouth puckering, his eyes staring straight ahead, as befitted the son of a politician of dreams. "Gawd," he groaned under his breath, "I wish dad was here."

At last our case was called. We walked up near the judge, who gave us no more attention than if we had been ants in the forest. He was not paid to use imagination, and he had no time to think about the environmental forces that had placed us before him. There was one thing to solace me – a pickpocket had said that all the jails in the district were crowded, and that if I put up a good line of talk, "His Nibs" would dismiss our case.

The railroad detective told in detail how he had captured us sound asleep in an empty box car. He stood near me, his eyes like little black beads, crowding near a swollen, hooked nose that spread across his face. He told the judge that many cars had been broken into, and that the railroad wished the coöperation of the district in apprehending the offenders.

When he had finished, at a nod from the judge, I talked in our defence. Baltimore had recently burned, and the disaster gave wings to my imagination. We were on our way there to work as rivet heaters. We had no money. We had been forced to tramp from Chicago. I told of the wild ride across the mountains, and of the clinging to the one train from Cincinnati. The judge listened, slightly less bored, and possibly seeing through the lies. He looked at a small mallet which he held in his hand, then about the court room, and at us again, and said, "I'll give you boys until to-night to leave town. Case dismissed. Next."

There followed pleasant hours on a slow freight the forty odd miles to Baltimore. We begged a meal from fishermen on Chesapeake Bay.

A detective disputed the right of way with us in Wilmington, and in our haste to leave him in full possession, I fell over a railroad tie and rolled nearly to Philadelphia.

The echo of Dutch's laugh could be heard above the roar of a passenger train. "Laugh, you damn fool," I said.

"I am laughing," he replied. "Wouldn't you?"

We reached Philadelphia early in the morning, and walked through the quiet city, mile after weary mile. Whole streets seemed to be built exactly alike, as though the one brain had planned them all. As red-brick flat building merged into the other one, the white front steps, exactly alike on each, glared in the early morning sun. Green shutters were on each building, attached to which, we found out later, were looking-glasses which gave the flat-dweller a view of the street below.

Bottles of milk, newspapers, and sometimes loaves of bread could be seen at the front doors.

The milk was very tempting. Dutch picked up a bottle from one door, and I picked up a bottle from the next one. Dutch then picked up a loaf of bread and a newspaper. We started to walk hastily away, when a voice yelled, "Hey there!" We looked up suddenly and saw a man leaning out of a second-story window. A looking-glass, fastened to a shutter, slanted down toward the front door. We ran swiftly away, and turned the first corner at a terrific pace, without putting on brakes at all.

Two policemen stood near a lamp post, and Dutch bumped into one of them. There was a frightful roar from the guardian of the law. He sprawled on his hands and knees. The milk fell with a crash, and painted the blue trousers and big black shoes of the other policeman with a smear of white. Dutch held to the bread and rolled, while I ran. Suddenly I heard the patter of feet coming closer and closer. Every moment I expected the pursuing policeman to grab me. All of a sudden a form shot by me. "Come on," Dutch yelled. "Follow me." Mortified, I ran after the squat, bowlegged Hollander.

The loaf of bread was crunched under his arm. The newspaper was crumpled in his right hand. He was bareheaded, and his yellow hair stood straight up on his cone-shaped head.

The paper top came out of the bottle I carried, and I held my hand over it to save the milk that remained. Dutch turned into an alley, and I followed him. We stopped, breathed loud and long, and then laughed.

"I'll bet that bull thought an elephant hit him," grinned Dutch.

Having eaten the bread, we hurried to the Pennsylvania Railroad. Before long a freight train came, and we scrambled into an empty coal car. Trenton had the reputation of being a "hostile" town. It was about half way between New York and Philadelphia. We sat in the car as the train bumped along, and worried about a bridge before we had crossed it. Many tales had been told us about the "bad bull" who was in Trenton. He had beaten a hobo unconscious.

The sun blazed into the open car, and, weary with the troubles of the road, we became drowsy and finally slept.

We awoke in the middle of the afternoon, as the train stood still. A young boy walked near the car. Dutch yelled to him, "Say, kid, where are we?"

"Newark," was the answer.

"Gosh," said the relieved Dutch, "we pounded our ear right through Trenton."

We left the train in the yards at Jersey City, and finally reached New York as the sun went down.

New York had been our faint objective, but after reaching there we suddenly decided to tramp to New Haven, Connecticut. Some vagrant had told Dutch that Yale students often gave away fine suits of clothes.

We dreamed of new clothes and the generosity of Yale students. I had the notion then that all college students were the sons of wealthy men.

We begged our supper and the fare to New Rochelle. There, with the gnawing hunger of the day banished, we waited for a freight on the New York, New Haven, and Hartford Railroad.

As we waited, another young tramp joined us. He was bound for a town in Rhode Island where a street fair was in progress.

Instead of waiting for the freight, we walked to the depot with the new-found rover, and boarded a mail train bound for Boston.

We reached Kingston, R. I., in the early morning, and had breakfast at our fellow traveller's expense in a dingy all-night railroad restaurant.

Before the natives started to flock to the fair booths, we had secured a position. A young man from New York who had the concession to run an "if-you-win-you-lose game," engaged us as "come-on guys."

The contraption was made like a slender suit case. It rested upon a tripod in the manner of a camera. Little marbles ran through a forest of steel pegs, and the natives would bet that the marbles would light on certain colored spots. The young man controlled a lever. Strangely, the marbles never lit on the spots which the natives picked.

Each of the "come-on guys" was given five dollars with which to gamble. The citizens, seeing them win money, would try and try again and again. When the money was won, an accompliee would walk through the crowd and collect it.

A young farmer lost twenty-seven dollars. With more courage than prudence, he hit the young man from New York in the jaw.

That gentleman stepped from behind the contraption, as debonair as a clerk who wished to show a ribbon. His hands moved forward quickly, and the young farmer sank, a crumpled heap, on the ground.

A commotion started. A confederate closed the contraption and walked away with it. I became excited, but Dutch had more caution.

"This ain't our fight," said he. "Let's breeze on out."

I had three dollars which I had not gambled, and Dutch had four. In our haste to leave, we completely forgot to return the money to the young man who had handled his fists so gracefully.

That evening we were bound in the direction of New Haven.

The rover of the night before had cautioned us against New Haven. "There's a big bull there, and he has a big St. Bernard dog. They meets all the fast trains early in the evenin'. You git off on one side, the dog gits you. On the other side, the bull nabs you." We had climbed upon the roof the night before, and had stretched out silently all the time the train was at the station in the college town. Night and the train reached New Haven together. We left the blind baggage hurriedly, and circled about until we reached the other side of the station. We then waited for the train to leave.

As it steamed out, we ran swiftly toward the engine. A rough voice yelled, "Halt!"

I squatted low, and kept on going. A dog barked viciously as it bounded over the tracks. It looked as big as a cow. A hand grasped the tail of my coat. I jerked it off quickly, but held to the iron ladder. A man rolled backward from the train with my coat in his hands. The dog barked loudly. The engine shrieked, and slowed down. For a heart-sickening moment, I thought the train would stop. Things happened quickly. I looked back and saw Dutch jump over a switch light, the dog after him. A man grabbed Dutch.

I muscled my body to the top of the mail car, and went on my hands and knees the full length of the train as it left the yards.

From the rear car I could see two men, a dog, and Dutch. The train, which moved slowly to give the detectives a chance to "frisk" it, now speeded up.

Months later I met Dutch. He had stayed ninety days in New Haven, as a guest of the city. During that time, he wore a suit, not given him by a Yale student. He worked on a rock pile for three months.

I journeyed on alone, my thoughts keeping pace with the rapid clicking of the wheels upon the rails. High above, the stars swung. A battalion of white clouds formed in the south and marched steadily up the sky. They turned darker and disappeared, rumbling all the while. I held to the small pipe that ran along the roof, as the cars swayed under the smoke from the engine that trailed over the train. A blinding flash of lightning streaked through the clouds that now hid the swinging stars. A roar followed as of trains crashing together.

Forgetful of all but the weird, wild beauty of the scene, I lay, a young Irish rover, and gazed steadily upward. The rain suddenly spattered on the roof like broken pearls. A wind whirled over the train that now lurched through the wet, dark night like a huge dragon mad with fear. The lightning flared again and made the car-roof glisten green. I started to crawl from under the windswept rain. I slipped and grabbed at the pipe as the train swerved. I lay still. For some moments longer, there was no let up to the fury of the breeze and the rain. I envied the railroad bull my coat as the wind lashed through my shirt with the sting of a rawhide whip, while I lay face downward and held to the small pipe with aching hands.

The rain stopped. The clouds separated a moment, and the stars peeked through them. Turning white, they travelled swiftly over the sky like great billows across a blue and star-specked ocean. They merged together again, and turned steel grey, then black. The sky was completely hidden.

Choosing rather to be lashed by the rain than to crawl across the wet and speeding train, I made no move.

The train dashed through a small town as the rain fell upon it. The engine screeched for a crossing and in a moment we were in the open country again.

The cold air numbed my muscles until a stupor fought to gain control of my brain. Silently I fought with a primitive lust for life. I pounded the roof of the car to revive the ebbing circulation of my blood. I slapped my forehead with a free hand. I shook my head violently, as a pugilist does to drive the effect of a grueling smash from his brain. I longed for the train to stop. I thought of a lad who had been riding the "top" when the train speeded under a low bridge. It threw him far from the train, with a crushed skull, into the last oblivion that comes to tramp and king.

Distorted fancies crowded into my head, but still the rain beat down. The water soaked through my cap and plastered it to my hair like a wet rag.

On and on the train rolled, the whistle of the engine being barely heard above the roar of the cars, the shrieking of the wind, and the mad patter of the rain.

At last it came to the lighted edge of a town. The speed of the train slackened. It stopped at a depot, near which steel rails glistened white in the rainy night.

I climbed down the rear end of the last car with aching hands and body.

Walking slowly away from the depot, I came to an abandoned shed in which many old newspapers were scattered. Removing my clothes, I rubbed my body vigorously, and then wrapped the newspapers around me.

I slept on the bare floor in this fashion.

When morning came, my clothing was nearly dry.

I begged a coat several sizes too large for me, and went into New York with what remained of the young gambler's money.

CHAPTER XXI
A SWITCH IS THROWN

FOR TWO WEEKS, I stayed in New York, living as a bird lives, though not as carefree. At times, I cursed the wanderlust that held me in its grip. While cursing, I loved it. For it gave me freedom undreamed of in factories, where I would have been forced to labor.

I then went through a long siege as a hobo in the Central States.

Snow fell at a water tank in Cairo, a tri-state town at the edges of Missouri, Kentucky, and Illinois. Nearly thirty tramps were there, the dishevelled of the earth. Some carved their monikers on the red-painted pine boards. Others talked of the road – always the road. Some read yellow magazines and old newspapers. For current things have no especial value in tramp life. The days of the week or month have no importance for tramps either.

I was travelling alone, and waited for a mail train to stop at the tank. Experience of the road told me that so many would be unable to ride the one train south. So I sauntered a train length away from the water tank. By avoiding the flagman at the rear I might be able to "top" the train to Memphis.

The light from the engine flared down the track, as the train passed me and stopped for water. When the flagman had walked a hundred yards to the rear, I clambered on top of the train.

The roofs of mail and passenger cars are slanting, and it requires steady nerves and acquired experience to walk upon them as they rush over the ground. A small ship in a storm is a smooth board walk in comparison.

The train pulled slowly out amid many shouts. The crew was at war with the tramps. When the rear car passed the tank, I saw them in disappointed numbers looking at the disappearing train. Hoping that I would encounter no tunnels or low bridges along the road, I crawled slowly the length of the train until I came to the first blind. I then jumped from the first car to the coal tender and watched the changing scenery from a seat on an empty tool box.

Fulton was reached with no trouble. As the train left Fulton, I saw from my hiding-place behind a post, two men board the first blind. I had a hunch, from their self-confident manner, that they were railroad detectives. The snow fell slowly in tiny flakes. Neither wishing to crawl over the train again, nor to lie shivering and dejected on top of it, I watched it fade toward the Tennessee city.

Within an hour, as is often the case, a merchandise train followed the limited out of Fulton. Could the two "bulls" be riding down the line in order to wait for the merchandise freight? I wondered. As there are twenty chances of beating a freight to one on a mail train, I decided to try.

I succeeded in eluding the watchful eyes of the train crew, and boarded the manifest train. It was too cold for the crew to stay outside, so, while the train kept running, I had it to myself. After a short time on the bumpers, I climbed on top and tried the different hatchways in the tops of the cars. At last I came to one that was not sealed.

This I opened, and found empty. Below the hatchway was an airtight, zinc-enclosed box. I crawled inside and burned newspapers to raise the temperature.

With uneasy mind, I pictured my fate should a brakesman seal the door. With such pleasant thoughts, I fell into a troubled sleep.

When I awoke and raised the door above me, broad day streaked in, and my heart pounded light. I crawled outside and stood on the bumpers of the running train. In this manner I reached Memphis.

The snow had vanished, and in its place, cinders from the engine rained upon the roofs of the cars.

It was a muggy day and the southern wind gnawed to the bone. Coffee was the uppermost thing in my mind, and I entered a Greek restaurant, with an old trick in view. Greeks were not considered kindly disposed toward beggars, but I would try and make one of the diners hear my request for food.

The Greek owner turned my request down flat, but loud. A bleareyed individual sat at the horseshoe counter and smeared his chin with the yellow of an egg. He looked my way. Now every "road-kid" knows that forty-nine out of every fifty drunkards will feed him. If it were a drunken world, the beggars would own it.

I walked over to the drunkard, who seemed slow in comprehending. He listened a moment, and said, "What's you want?" A Greek flunky came near. "Ham an' eggs," I said.

The drunkard talked, while I listened attentively, as became a beggar of food. I agreed with him thoroughly, and marveled at his wisdom. Running in the back of my head were not the things he was saying. I was wondering if he would give me some money. After I listened to his maudlin talk for an hour, the inebriated scoundrel only gave me twenty-five cents.

I bade the ungrateful man goodbye, and hurried from the place to the Arkansas side of the river, near Bridge Junction. The freight trains did not stop there, unless by an unforeseen chance. Glowing pleasantly with food and drink, my courage ran high. I spied a man sitting alone in the tower, and walked up the steps to him.

Hoboes in railroad towers are as rare as preachers in Heaven. But I thought not of that. With a quickness born of the road, I allowed the man to talk of that which pleased him.

He had a mania for showing his brothers the light. And I was a young sinner far from home. While listening to his exhortations, I watched the levers that controlled the interlocking system, and noticed that the switch near the main track was a "hand switch," and was not controlled by the levers in the tower.

Night came suddenly without twilight.

The headlight of an engine could be seen at least a mile away. The switch light below gave it a clear track. It drew rapidly nearer, and, knowing it would be impossible to catch the train at the terrific rate of speed it was travelling, I bade the man good-night as coolly as possible and hurried down the steps. I hid in the dark for a few brief seconds, and then rushed toward the switch.

Many forms came out of the darkness. The tower guardian rushed down the steps into the arms of danger. As I touched the switch, a heavy hand pushed me backward. The tower-man hurried forward. A fist rapped him on the jaw. He fell quickly and lay still.

Chapter XXII
Burned Out

THE FORMS VANISHED into the darkness, and I rushed after them.

The air was applied amid a grinding of noise. Then engineer and firemen leaned out of the cab, while the head brakeman stood low on the iron ladder of the first car, his light swinging furiously as the train curved on the side track.

The crew ran toward the engine, while we glided like phantoms in the same direction, far out of sight of the crew.

The train men talked excitedly, and a rough voice asked loudly in the dark, "Who the hell threw that switch?"

I crowded near a box car with many others. A door was slid noiselessly open and eighteen of us crawled inside. The door was shut and fastened from within.

A tramp lit a match. It was knocked out of his hand. "No glim now, you fool," hissed another.

A nervous quiet came. A man stepped on a paper. It rattled loudly. "Shhh," a voice purred.

We listened to our own hearts beat. Presently steps could be heard outside. The door was tried. It did not give. "I'd like to git hold of the rats, who threw that switch," a voice could be heard saying.

After a seemingly endless time, the train started on. No move was made until the noise of it drowned out all other sounds. Then matches lit cigarettes and pipes, and blurred into the bearded faces of as motley a gang of hoboes as ever rode a freight.

The car was soon filled with smoke as dense as an ocean fog. The odour of unkempt bodies filled the airless place, until a tramp unfastened the door.

A cold wind blew into the car. The door was shut again. There followed much coughing, and the door was again opened.

A tramp peered out. A light streamed back from the engine, as the fireman shovelled coal in the open fire box.

"We're in a swamp on a trustle," the hobo said.

She's miles long, an' deeper'n hell. I've been over it."

Another light showed the cat-tails waving in the cold wind.

The temperature became colder. The wind blew over the swamp and penetrated our thinly clad bodies. The door was closed again, and the stifling air clogged our lungs.

"Open 'er up some. We'll build a fire. May's well burn to death as freeze to death." I glanced at the speaker and vaguely connected him with the wielder of the fist that had knocked the keeper of the tower sprawling.

He was heavily built. His hands were large, like hams, and they reached nearly to his knees. His face, once good looking, was now stamped with a vicious leer. His mouth was firm, and slanted slightly downward at the left edge. His eyes were shot with blood, and the lids were red. His hair fell in straggly red masses over his ears and neck. His coat was torn and gaped like wounds under his armpits. A lighted cigarette was in the left corner of his mouth. The upper lip did not seem to touch it, and it hung down, the lighted end nearly touching the red stubble of his beard.

His short neck bulged under his ears. They looked strangely white in the tangled mass of red hair around them.

There was decision and mastery about him. Boy lover of raw strength, I watched him.

"Who's the guy?" I asked a tramp near me.

"Oklahoma Red," he answered, and then lower, and more drawn out, "He's a b-a-d g-u-y."

"A couple of you guys come with me," said Red. "We'll crawl over the rattler an' hunt some wood." He sprang up, turned backward, and fastened his big hands on the roof of the rolling car. The open places under his armpits gaped wider as his muscular body swung upward on the roof. Then his feet were heard tramping overhead.

Two other men followed him, and presently boxes and boards were hurled into the car. The three men followed them.

Some of the wood was prepared in a jiffy, and soon a fire was blazing in the car. The men huddled around, and as their bodies thawed, their tongues loosened. A man peered out again, and jerked his head back. "We'll never git out o' this damned swamp," he said.

The men talked in animated fashion while the fire ate its way through the floor and fell on the track below.

Another fire was built in an oily spot at the other end of the car. It burned slowly at first, while we huddled around it. "Watch she don't git away from us," advised a tramp.

"We give a damn," said Oklahoma Red. "We'll burn up the damn train an' take the caboose."

"That's us," said a one-legged man, whom the crowd called Peg-leg.

The blaze spread and crept over the floor and up the sides of the car to the roof. "Let 'er burn, Hurray!" yelled a voice.

The fire worked its way to the door. "She's hot enough now," said Peg-leg. The whistle shrieked for a town, while all ears listened. Red swung the end door back as the flames became hotter. He crawled out, the rest of us after him. Peg-leg used his crutch with dexterous grace.

The flame lit up the landscape as we jumped from the train. As the car went on, it became darker, and we lay flat on the ground until the caboose passed. We then circled into the open country and watched the train stop in the small town.

Lanterns swung together, and the engine whistle gave a wild shriek as men hurried from both ends of the train to the burning car. It was hurriedly cut from the train and placed on a sidetrack. The shouting of the crew could be heard distinctly. In a short time, there was a loud noise as the roof of the car caved in.

The crowd scattered, some refusing to ride the train again.

Oklahoma Red, Peg-leg, two other tramps, and myself were in the mood to ride toward Little Rock. We hurried ahead of the train, Peg-leg easily keeping pace with us.

"Kin you ketch 'er?" asked one of the tramps of Peg-leg.

"Sure," he replied. "I kin git 'er goin' twenty miles an hour."

A swiftly running man could not catch a train going much faster. We were astonished and doubtful of Peg-leg's statement.

Feeling that the crew would be on the lookout for tramps after the incident of the burning car, we walked far enough ahead of the train to make them feel that it was impossible for the most daring of hoboes to catch it.

There was no moon visible, and, save for the light which travelled from the engine in a straight line, the night was as black as coal.

The engine climbed a slight elevation and puffed with fury.

It gained speed and rolled down the elevation, while we waited far out in the dark.

As it approached us, Oklahoma Red said, "Git on first, kid, an' you, Peg. We'll make it then."

I ran swiftly with the train, Oklahoma Red behind me. A gondola came alongside of us. "Git in here. We'll come." It was a daring moment. I ran along and grasped the iron ladder. Peg-leg was ahead of me, and the redoubtable Red had somehow reached him.

But Peg-leg needed no assistance. Though all of fifty years old, he clutched the rung of the iron ladder I had climbed, his wooden leg sticking out from the car like the end of an immense broom stick. Some cans rattled in a bundle which was flung across his shoulder.

In a short time, another tramp and Oklahoma Red joined us. "Where's the other fellow?" I asked.

"Guess he couldn't make it," answered Peg-leg.

The gondola in which we rode contained a long steam boiler. The wind whistled through the many holes in it, and made it rumble like a piano when a hand is jerked lightly over it.

"It's colder'n hell with the door open," said Oklahoma Red. "There's a brick yard in Bald Knob. We'll get off there. What do you say?"

"Sure," we answered.

We left the train in the early morning, as the train neared Bald Knob.

The banked fires in the brick yard glowed cherry red. Clouds raced westward as the sky cleared in the east. The train travelled on, and all became still. A rooster crowed several times and became silent.

We sat near a furnace and dozed. Men's voices floated faintly across the yard to us.

"There's a jungle down the line a short ways," said Red. "That's the 'boes you hear talkin'."

"Let's beat it there," suggested Peg-leg, who sat, his hard face battered by storms, his eyes, still soft, and gazing at the red slabs of clay.

Near him was the bundle which he carried, a shoe projecting out of the dirty canvas.

"What do you carry the other shoe for?" I asked.

"Because it saves me bummin' shoes all the time," he answered, laughing. Then, as if in confidence, "I kin allus tell when it's goin' to rain, too. The stub end o' my leg aches. Darn handy, huh?"

"How'd you lose your foot?" asked someone.

"None o' your business," snapped Peg-leg in the tone of a man who kept a secret.

"I'll bet you wore it off runnin' from some railroad bull," laughed Red, as he scratched his mane of red hair.

"Naw, I was swimmin' in Frisco Bay, an' a boat run over it," grunted Peg-leg resuming his gaze at the fire.

CHAPTER XXIII
THE JUNGLE

WE WALKED TO THE JUNGLE where we found many hoboes. It was situated near a running brook. The gathering of derelicts made us welcome, and asked news of the road. Some treated Oklahoma Red with rude courtesy.

"Mulligan ready?" asked Red. "We're hungrier'n wolves."

"Sure thing, old yegger," answered a shrivelled tramp whose body shook as he walked.

A half dozen fires burned, and hoboes worked like army cooks over them. Some brought water from the creek, while others peeled potatoes, and prepared meat for the skillets.

The men were divided in groups, and talked in the argot of the road.

The camp was plentifully supplied. "You sure got some grub here," said Red to the shrivelled tramp. "Yeah, an' we sure shook our legs to git it. We darn near bummed the whole country for what we didn't buy."

"What you didn't buy is good," said Oklahoma Red. "I'll bet you didn't buy none of it."

"Yes we did. Everybody's flush," was the answer. "We stole two barrels of corn juice from a nigger too."

The sun arose and shone for a short time, then disappeared behind dark clouds. They hung low, their black drapery nearly touching the trees that bordered the creek.

Hoboes stood on rocks in the brook, and washed themselves. Towels of every size and colour stretched on a wire from one tree to another.

A large, jagged piece of broken mirror was fastened to a tree with nails. A hobo stood in front of it, shaving himself with a piece of glass. The man's face bled in several places. When the glass removed a portion of beard and lather from his face, he would toss it deftly from him. When he had finished, he walked to the creek and knelt on a rock and buried his bleeding face in the running water.

Another hobo stood, with lathered beard, waiting. He picked up the glass and used it more deftly than the first rover, and when he had finished, his face was bloodless and smooth. He wiped it with a soiled red handkerchief, and walked over to a table, and began eating.

Many rude little make-believe houses stood near each other at the edge of the jungle. They were built out of railroad ties, and had three sides and a roof. The other side was completely open.

Under a large tree was what remained of a barrel of corn juice. A few men had sampled it in the early morning, but, for the most part, the tramps had been busily engaged in preparing breakfast.

A man with both legs off sat near the barrel of liquor. His crutches stood near a tree, against which he leaned. He held a tin cupful of the white fluid in his hand. He was bitter at the world. The injustice of it rankled him. "Country's gone to seed," he said. "Salvation Army gits a license to beg in Little Rock, an' I can't. No use bein' crippled no more. Country's bound for hell in a handbasket." He stopped talking and gurgled the white fluid.

It began to rain. The drops fell suddenly and swiftly from the dark coulds and rattled in the tin dishes on the table. They played a rat-a-tat-tat on the bottom of a dishpan, that lay, rusty and battered, in an open space. The remaining leaves on the trees were beaten to the ground with water. A furious wind came up and clattered the tin dishes across the jungle. They rattled against the sides of trees and fell on the ground. The legless man dropped his empty cup and, grabbing his crutches, hurried away to the shelter of a three-sided house. His body swung on top of the crutches.

In a short time the open jungle was clear of tramps, and all were seated in the houses made of ties.

A young negro tramp arrived in the rain, carrying a "please don't rain" suitcase made out of pasteboard. As he moved across the open space in full view of the hoboes, the case crumpled up like a wet paper sack. The bottom and the sides dropped away, leaving the bedraggled, black vagabond standing, soaked with rain, and holding all that was left of the case in his hands, – the handle, the hinges, and the clasps.

A roar went up from the sheltered tramps, as the negro hurled the remnants of the suitcase from him. "Uncle Mose cheated you, boy. The kike saw you comin'," yelled a voice.

Soon the rain ran through the cracks in the roofs of ties, and the water poured inside as if from sieves. A pool formed in the centre of the jungle, and as the raindrops fell into it with a splash they resembled tiny masted ships sinking away forever. Every object became drenched with rain. The clothes of the shivering tramps dripped with water. There was no escape. Miserable men they were, the shabby tricksters of life. But they endured, like stoics, with a smile. They took what life, or the elements sent them. They fought and they drank; they begged and they robbed. But this can be written to their everlasting credit above the stars in the farthest sky – they did not whine.

The wind veered suddenly and drove the falling water into the open sides of the wretched shelters.

Peg-leg sat near me, watching the raindrops sink in the pool. There was a cleft in his nose between the eyes, and a drop of rain stood on it as if not daring to roll downward. He rubbed it away with his hand. "Nigger kicked me there one time," he said, "long before I lost my leg."

"Did you get him for it?" I asked.

"Damn near killed him. He yelled out loud for God. The black devil." That was all of the story. He became silent again, and stared at the falling raindrops.

Oklahoma Red sat quietly, his hair dripping wet.

"Any licker in that barrel?" he asked of the shrivelled tramp who sat near him.

"There was," came back the shivering answer. "Lots of the 'boes come in late, an' didn't know it was there."

Red stood up. "Come on, Peg. You too, Kid," he said.

We started for the barrel, then Red hesitated, and looking up at the slightly lighter sky, "It's clearin' up," he said.

The men offered me the cup first and I drank enough of the liquor to set my body tingling underneath its dripping clothes. Then Red and Peg-leg helped themselves generously, drinking several cups each, like sweating labourers at a well.

More hoboes left the houses and gathered about the barrel. A giant negro came close and swallowed a cupful of liquor. He reached down to fill the cup again. "What you think it is, your birthday?" asked a vagrant standing near.

"I guess I done stole this licka," answered the negro, "an' I got some moah stashed ovah yondah," pointing to a woods.

"How much more?" asked Red.

"Half a bah'l," replied the negro. "Anybody'll go 'long, ah'll go an' git it."

Two men volunteered, and the three walked through the mud in the direction of the woods.

Presently they returned, carrying the liquor between them.

"That's better'n a stove to warm us up," laughed Peg-leg, as several men adjusted the liquor in a secure place near the now nearly empty barrel.

"How'd you come to git the booze?" asked the legless man, who had just joined the crowd.

"I knows wheah a niggah had a still. De still ain' still theah no moah," answered the negro. "We done cleaned it up."

The clouds faded swiftly away, and the sun threw long shafts of light through the moist air.

Many of the vagrants walked in the direction of the brick yard with the hope of drying their clothes. Others stood, oblivious of wet rags so long as the corn liquor made their beggars' blood dance warm.

Unable to wait for the cups that passed around, some of the tramps made three-cornered cups out of papers still wet with rain.

The giant negro stealer of the liquor became loquacious under its influence. "Ah's been t'ree times 'cross dis country lookin' for a job, an' I ain't done found it yit," he said. "I kain't wuk at ma trade all year roun' nohow."

"What is your trade?" asked the legless man, who balanced himself on his crutches and held a cup in each hand.

"Ah's a Christmas tree decoratah," was the laughing answer of the negro, his teeth showing white and even in a mouth as large as the cave of a fairy.

The liquor was fast disappearing, and the men crowded about the barrels like hogs around a trough.

The giant negro stood, his legs outstretched, his big feet imbedded in the mud, a hollow black statue, never filled.

Oklahoma Red edged toward the barrel and placed his elbow in the negro's ribs and pushed him away.

"Wha's 'amatter, nigger. Think ye're alone?"

The negro's eyes flashed as he crowded near the barrel again. "Guess ah stole this licka," he shouted as he pushed Red away.

Battle started. Red, a foot shorter than the negro, shot upward with each fist, and the thud of his hands on the giant's jaws could be heard across the jungle.

The negro's head twisted on his neck. He stepped backward, and threw his coat in the face of a tramp before rushing in.

"Lord, he's got a razor," yelled Peg-leg.

"Keep still, you bum. Want the bulls out here?" snapped another hobo.

Oklahoma Red circled aobut until he had his back to the sun. His ponderous arms were in front of him, pugilist fashion. His jaws clamped as he moved his immense shoulders.

The negro charged, holding the razor even with Red's throat. Red kept his eye on the blade, the set look never leaving his face. The black man drew nearer and swished the razor through the air within six inches of Red's throat.

The latter's left hand drove like an iron weight a few inches below the blade. The razor turned in the negro's hand, and, driven backward by the blow, it slashed his cheek wide open. Red's right hand circled like a man throwing a ball. It covered the bleeding face of the now pain-mad negro, and the blood spurted several feet.

It was all done in the flash of an eye. The razor fell in the mud, and the negro crumpled near it, a broken, black mass, the whites of his eyes protruding from his dark and bloody face.

Blood oozed from the cheek, which fell away from his face.

He stretched unconscious on the wet and muddy ground. Red rubbed the blood from his big hands and sneered down at the still figure. "That'll do for you, you black devil. Anyone else?"

A rock sang through the air and caught Red on the jaw. He staggered back as three negroes rushed at him.

Peg-leg stood in the way of one negro and leaned low. His fist travelled upward and caught the rushing black in the centre of the groin. He bellowed like a calf, as his hands went down to the injured part of his body. He fell in a half-upright position on the ground. His head went forward and hit the empty barrel, which rolled down over his body. Peg-leg stepped nearer to him and swung his wooden leg, like a club, at his jaw. It tore the flesh from it. The negro lay still.

A hobo jumped on the back of another negro and applied the "strong arm," his right arm locking like a vise under the black's chin as it circled around his neck. He was dragged to the ground and choked until he could not move.

Red was evenly matched with another black. They tore the upper clothing from each other's bodies. In the negro's eyes was the expression of a black sheep, seared into battle with a lion, but he fought hard. Red rushed him into the crowd, fighting furiously.

The shrivelled tramp kicked the negro's shin. His mouth flew open as he yelled, "Oouh." It closed quickly as a blackjack crashed on his head. He fell forward on his face.

Oklahoma Red noticed the startled black carrier of the suitcase. "Hey you," he yelled, "take care o' your nigger brothers. Hear me!"

The scared darky said, "Yes sah, yes sah."

Peg-leg stood near Red. "I think I broke the nigger's jaw near the barrel," he said.

"Hope you did," returned Red, "but git me his shirt an' coat. Mine's gone to hell."

Peg-leg stripped the unconscious negro from his waist up, and brought the garments to Red. "We'd better beat it, hadn't we?" asked Peg-leg.

"I'll say so," replied Red. "Let's go."

Hoboes scattered in all directions, and I hurried away with Peg-leg and Red.

CHAPTER XXIV
OKLAHOMA RED

THROUGH THE COUNTRY, and over the railroad which we now hoboed, there were no fast trains worthy of the name. In such a country, particularly if it is "hostile," one incident often crowds upon another.

I waited for a freight train with Oklahoma Red and Peg-leg near a clump of shrubbery along the track. The train would be forced to climb a small hill at this point, which would retard its speed, a fact of which we were well aware.

After waiting some hours, we finally succeeded in riding a train to Little Rock.

As Oklahoma Red was not strictly a tramp, but a yegg, he had money. A yegg is a robber, a blower of safes, the aristocrat of the road, and the most dangerous man who travels it.

We had a meal at Red's expense in a railroad restaurant where Peg-leg met a hobo acquaintance who told him that Hot Springs was "good hittin'" generous at the time with beggars.

He at once decided to go to the health resort town, about fifty miles away. With a quick farewell, his wooden leg pounding on the rough floor, he passed out of our sight forever.

We lingered for a time in the restaurant, and then left for the railroad yards. The negro's coat fitted Red very tightly in the shoulders, but it was far too long for him.

The afternoon wore away, but still no freight train came.

Red became restless and went in search of liquor.

He soon returned with a full quart.

The colours faded from the west. The night became crystal clear. The moon rose, an immense mass of red and yellow, as large as the morning sun.

Red smoked innumerable cigarettes, and now and then took a great gulp of whiskey. I could hear it rattling down his throat like water over stones.

Oklahoma Red was the type of drinker who never staggered. His crude, strong mind controlled the brutal and life-scarred body until sheer exhaustion set in. He would then drop in his tracks.

Like most men of leisure, the hobo is fond of good liquor.

When prohibition came to our beloved land, he suffered greatly, but, being a keen observer, he found a way out. He became a member of what is now known as the "Sterno Club." In other words, a member of the "canned heat brigade." Sterno is a commercial product which is sold in cans and used for artificial heat. It is made of wood alcohol and parafine. These cans vary in sizes and can be bought at prices ranging from ten to fifty cents. Now, when the hobo wants a thrill, he buys a can of Sterno and mixes it in a concoction that would knock a mule out. As a rule, he buys the cheaper cans in the ten-cent stores. He empties the contents, oftimes in a dirty kerchief, and squeezes it until the wood alcohol has been extracted from the parafine. He then mixes the alcohol with soda pop, or some other such ingredient, and drinks it. One good drink is enough to send even a Baptist minister to oblivion for a day. Hoboes buy cans of Sterno in large numbers and take them to the "jungles." It is no uncommon sight to see them stretched upon the ground, the débris of intoxication all around them.

The silence was upon me, and I refused to talk. Red grew weary of his own thoughts. "Where you from, Kid?" he asked.

I shot back an answer which I hoped would keep him quiet. "I'm from everywhere but here, and I'll be from here soon."

He ignored my attempt at smartness. "I'm from Aurland," he said. "Dublin."

"Gosh," I answered, with slightly roused interest, "I thought you was from this country."

"Nope. But I've been here since I was seventeen."

Red's eyes were half closed. His hat was on the back of his head, and the red hair straggled over his forehead in a tangled mass of curls.

Starved for affection through all the rough years of my short life –
my heart went out to him. He was kind. He gave me all he had and
asked nothing in return.

I put my hand on his shoulder, "What'sa matter, Red? You look
blue."

"Naw, I ain't blue. I guess I'm half drunk. That nigger sure had me
thinkin' for a minit. That razor looked like a butcher knife. But I got
him squintin' at the sun. D' you notice. Whenever you fight a nigger,
Kid, keep lookin' right'n his eye. It'll git his goat ev'ry time."

"You kin fight like a house afire," I said. "Where'd you learn it?"

"You been on the road's long's I have, Kid, an' you'll have to fight."

"How long you been hittin' the grit, Red?"

"Since I was about five years old," he answered, as he removed his
hat and ran a big hand through his hair. He clamped his hat down on
his head, and again folded his arms and resumed his old position.

"My dad was a beggar. The dirty devil. I ain't sure he was my dad.
Anyhow, he had me an' my kid sister before we could remember. He
might o' grabbed us up somewhere, some foundlin' home, or somethin'. A lot o' those old stiffs used to do that over there.

"He was the meanest old devil that ever went without a tail. I seen
him pull his hair out of his head in bunches.

"He used to play blind, an' he'd take us two kids with him, and he
had a sign he tied on our breasts. It said, 'Motherless.' We'd go along
singin' crazy songs about God an' Heaven. The old boy'd sing too.
That old devil had more stalls than a livery stable. He could play par-
alyzed till I've seen old women cry over him.

"We used to hit all the towns over there. The ol' guy a beggin' with
us kids, and gettin' stewed on the money.

"My sister was a good kid. I remember when she went away with
some fat old Jane who was dressed up like a nigger wench on circus
day. After she left, the old bum was drunk for a week. She was fourteen years old, an' I was twelve. He sold that kid to that old cat. I did-
n't see her for years after I'd been over here an' back ag'in."

"Where is she now?" I asked.

"Croaked. She died a hophead. Ravin' nuts." There was a long pause. Red rubbed his forehead and resumed, "She cried an' kissed me an' petted me when she left, but the old man said how nice we'd both have it, an' I could come to see her in her new home. I tried to find them later, but I never could. I'd swing on five gallows to kill that old man. I'd hold him out an' shake him to death like a rat. I'd make him half dead, an' I'd bury him an' let the buzzards peck at his eyes. I'd put lime in the centre of his head, an' let it eat all around it."

"Did you ever learn to read or write?" I asked.

"A little. A moll buzzer taught me in Boston. She worked wit' a gang o' dips, an' sported a little on the side. She was a good fellow. Smart too. I lost track of her when I got sent up for three years in Charleston. I made enough shoes there to last an army a year. I bumped into an old crook there, an I learned how to crack safes an' fix the ends o' my fingers so's they was sensitive to touch, by makin' 'em raw. I've done two jolts since that. Got ten years out west the last jolt, an' I broke a guard's jaw wit' one rap when he cracked me wit' a club.

"They put me in the Red Shirt Brigade after that. The bad guys had to wear red shirts all the time." A leer played into a cynical half smile on Red's face, as he stopped to light another cigarette.

"I got away from there, by God, red shirt and all. I walked every night for two weeks. Most guys when they make a gitaway, hang around some town where the bulls kin easy find them. I stayed right out on the road for a year straight. I never hung around no town at all. I let my hair an' beard grow, and turned no trick for a long time."

Red emptied the bottle with a long gulp, and dashed it against the steel rail.

"Stick with me, Kid. I'll treat you right. I git darn lonesome. I'll show you how to pour the juice and blow a safe so's it won't wake a baby. You won't have to run away from me like I did the old devil when I was a kid. I don't bum no back doors. I get mine. Most bums ain't got nerve enough to rob safes. Everybody's crooked anyhow. Everybody doublecrosses everybody else. They ain't nobody straight. I know they wantta git me. They got me mugged all over. But the guy that gits me, gits me dead. I'll start shootin'."

He pulled from his pocket a short blue gun that could be hidden in the palm of his hand. He looked at it a moment, his eyes narrowing.

"I'd like to shoot 'em all, Kid, but you an' me. They're all crooked. They let that old bum drag me around. Who the hell cared? I'm goin' to git even wit' 'em all. When any of the judges jolted me, they diden' say, 'Well, Kid, you diden' get a fair shake. They made you a crook an' they got mad because you are one. Then they sent cops worse than you are after you.' Judges are dummer than yeggs, believe me."

A light streamed from the yards. It blinded us for a moment, and then slanted away. With puffing of smoke and loud exhausts, the engine pulled a freight swiftly toward us. We stood erect, and Red tottered a little. We took our positions along the track, tense, like relay runners through a moonlit night.

Red yelled, "Grab her first, Kid." I ran with the train, and leaped on the iron ladder. I then looked around for Red.

He was dragging from the ladder of the second car behind me, his head bumping on the ties.

Brain benumbed and excited, I leaped from the train, and barely succeeded in keeping my footing. I hurried to Red. His foot had slipped through the rung of the ladder, which hung low on the car. I ran with the train and pulled his body loose.

It rolled away from the track, and I knelt over it. His arm was cut off at the elbow. It dripped, bloody and ghastly under the moon.

The train passed on. "Red!!" I yelled, and grabbed frantically at his breast. His heart stopped in a dying flutter. I sobbed aloud.

Dazed, I sat near him. As I watched, he seemed to smile. Many thoughts rushed across my mind... Would I tell anyone of his death? They might hold me. How about a burial? What was the difference? Did Red have money? The gun....

A stone rolled under his leg. It moved. A momentary fear came. I braced myself and looked at the dead face again.

Death had ironed his habitual leer away. The dead grey eyes stared up at the sky. Somehow, all the good in Red's bruised and broken life surged into his face. It was calm. The jolting of his head on the ground had thrown his long hair backward from his forehead. It showed, broad and white. Large bumps were across the eyes. Years later, I learned how wise men said that such bumps denoted great powers of observation. Anyhow, it was the forehead of a man born for greater things than being a member of a Red Shirt Brigade, and dying the death of a yegg along a railroad in Arkansas.

How long I remained with him I do not know. Faint and far away was the noise of the railroad yards. As one hour followed another into eternity, even that noise subsided. A passenger train rushed by. The lights from its coaches flickered over all that was mortal of Oklahoma Red.

The thought of Red's money came to me again. "If I don't get it the bulls will," I thought. I searched his pockets. There was but two dollars in them. Feeling that a man of Red's type would have more than that, I did not give up. I pulled off both his shoes. I searched every conceivable place I thought a man would sew his money who travelled among thieves – like detectives and tramps. I took the two dollars and blue gun. I walked away from Red, feeling that he would be found in the morning. And if he were not – what did it matter?

In a few hours I rode a freight past the place where he was lying dead. I sold the blue gun to a Jew in Dallas, who gave me four dollars for it. The money burned and I spent it quickly.

Oklahoma Red had a name to conjure with in yegg circles. I have met many who knew him, but I told them not of his death. I had the foolish notion that Red would not have cared for them to know.

CHAPTER XXV
AN EASY RIDE

AFTER THREE DAYS IN DALLAS, I hunted the railroad yards, penniless, as usual. Being young at the time, I thought often of Red.

It was a cold evening, and the frost was beginning to settle when I met an old vagrant near the railroad.

He told me that a "dead head" passenger coach was to leave for the west that night.

I thrilled at the idea of breaking into an empty coach where I might be able to ride on a plush seat all night, safe from the cold, and the eyes of shacks and bulls.

We talked of the road, and my old informant told me how he always wrapped paper around his legs for two useful purposes. Dogs could not bite through the paper, and it also helped to keep his worn shanks warm.

He was just getting over an injury. The door of a flat car had fallen upon his foot and had broken several bones in it. He had been unable to walk for a month, and was just beginning to venture about without a crutch. Still, he was bound for St. Louis.

Two women of the underworld had kept him in a small room, and had looked after him tenderly.

He spent much of his time near the yards watching the freight trains come and go. He gave each passing hobo the news about bulls, and the movements of trains.

I thought of those two women. "They're good scouts," I said.

"Sure," grunted the old hobo, "them kind are always good. They're down and out themselves a lot o' times." He looked at me thoughtfully, his faded old eyes half shut. "Yu ain't got a dime on yu, have yu, 'Bo?"

"Not a red cent."

"Yu're a hell of a bum," he ejaculated with contempt.

"Oh, well, you'll have a lot of jack when you hit St. Louis."

The old wretch grinned, and the crow's feet moved around his eyes. "Sure thing. I'll be rich when Rockyfeller an' me put our dough together."

It grew dark while we talked. The old rover again gave me the exact location of the train which contained the empty coaches. "It's straight," he said. "One of the girls knows a brakie, an' he told her. For two cents I'd go with yu, jist to git the nice ride on the cushions."

"St. Louis ain't that way," I answered.

"Well, that wouldn't make much difference," he sighed.

The night closed in around him as I walked away. The engine stood in the yards that was to haul the train west. I sneaked through the cars on the many tracks and hid behind a shed. A man joined me in the indistinct light.

"Makin' this train out, 'Bo?" he asked.

It flashed through my mind that he might be a detective, so I ignored the question. Vainly I tried to get a good look at his face to read there whether he was bull or bum. It can always be done by the observers of life on the road and in the underworld. The man-hunter has the look of one the wide world over.

No light flared distinctly. The engine stood puffing ahead of us.

Finally it began to travel backward, the brakeman standing on the rear, ready to connect it with the first car.

It made the ground vibrate near the shed as it rolled past it. The headlight flared in our direction. It shone directly in the face of the man with me. He was not a detective. He had the face of a dope-fiend. The light turned straight and we were in darkness again.

I began talking to my new-found companion. "We'd better beat it, 'Bo. The coach is in the middle of the train."

"I know, I know," he jerked back nervously, "let's go." We glided over the ground softly, stooping low, as if to take the weight from our feet. At last we stood panting between two cars opposite the coach. A lantern moved toward us.

We held our breath as it drew nearer. The swinger of it stopped within five feet of us. He held the lantern aloft and looked at the platform of the passenger coach. Had he listened close, he might have heard our hearts beat. They pounded loud in the silence.

Just at the moment, the coach was the most desired thing in my life. Years later, I delayed a journey because I could not get a Pullman berth. But here I was ready to knock a man out that I might ride on faded seats, in a dirty passenger car considered unfit for service on a third-class railroad. Of proverbs, rolling hackneyed down the ages, the truest of all is that "necessity knows no law."

The carrier of the lantern turned halfway around, and the light threw shadows between the cars. We stood as still as the rails beneath us. We could see the outline of the man's face and the corduroy cap on his head. He seemed nailed to the ground.

At last, whistling softly, he walked on between the cars in the direction of the caboose. After he was several car lengths from us, we darted on the platform of the coach. I looked up and down the other side of the train. A man stood near the caboose with a lantern. I watched him a moment. Presently the lantern "high-balled" a signal to the engine, and the air was applied. Two short whistles from the engine, the train jerked, and was on its way.

My companion tried the door. It held fast. He jerked out a key that grated in the lock. As the train sped by the lighted streets, he succeeded in opening the door. We crept inside.

The street lights flared across the seats. To our surprise, nearly every one of them contained a hobo. Some smoked, others talked, and some held their hands above their eyes and gazed out at the passing landscape.

My companion hurried to the other end of the car, and, saying no word, twisted himself in corkscrew fashion on an empty seat, and was soon grunting and snoring.

A hobo got up and tried the door, which we had left unlocked. He fastened it from the inside. "Them guys musta thought they has their fares paid," he grunted aloud.

I doubled up on a seat, and fell to wondering about my companion. I had heard of the daring of dope-fiends. He had a railroad key. I soon fell asleep.

A mumble of voices awoke me. It was broad daylight. The train pounded steadily over the rails as I rubbed my eyes and looked at the life-distorted faces of the men in the car.

They belonged to vagrants of all ages. There was one boy not much older than myself. His cheeks were hollow. He looked out of the window, listless, and oblivious of the passing scenery without, or the noise of the men within.

I watched him as he rose and walked to the water tank. There was no water. He swore at his luck.

A hobo sneered, "Yer wants service, huh? You got the wrong train."

"Shut yure head," flashed back the boy. "The flies'll crawl in." He returned to his seat, and fell to coughing.

Attracted by his age, boylike, I walked over to him.

"Where are we?" he asked indifferently.

"I don't know," I answered, and then shouted his question through the car.

"Runnin' into San Antone. They switched us on a faster rattler down the line. We're luckier'n tramps with hot biscuits an' java."

"The grades're gittin' heavier too," said another tramp.

We stopped at a small station and remained for some time. We pulled the curtains down, and sat speechless and quiet in the dark car.

A man tried the door knob. He stamped upon the coach platform for a short time, and went away. We heard his footsteps on the ground along the car.

When they died away, we breathed easier again. The train started. "Gosh, that was a close call. I'd hate to git ditched here," said a tramp.

After we reached the open country, the curtains were pulled up. No man had even the cheapest watch. I judged from the position of the sun that it was nearly noon. It seemed I had been a week on the train. It could not have been more than twenty hours.

"I wish I had a drink of water," murmured the youth.

We'll be in San Antonio before long. They'll put this car off there, sure," I said.

My companion of the night before kept aloof from the rest of the bleary gathering, and contented himself by talking aloud to people of his fancy who flew along with the train.

The men moved back and forth in restless manner. Some read old newspapers over and over again. Four men played poker with a dirty deck of cards, with matches and toothpicks for stakes. Another amused himself by cutting his moniker on the window sill. When he had finished, he stood up and admired it like an artist. An arrow was cut through the letters of his name. It pointed west, and denoted the direction in which he was travelling. The month and the year of the trip were cut beneath the name. These monikers are cut, written, or printed on water tanks and other places where hoboes gather. They form a crude directory for other tramps who might be interested in the itinerary of their comrades. Once in a while a tramp sees such a moniker of a friend and starts in the direction of the owner.

Growing tired of the youth, I walked back to my companion of the night before. He looked displeased, like a decrepit fanatic disturbed in prayer. He became more friendly after he had finished talking to an imaginary person who perched above him.

Late in the afternoon we reached San Antonio, and scampered out of the car as it came to the edge of the yards.

I hurried away across the tracks with the man of visions.

Chapter XXVI
The Man of Visions

WE HURRIED through the sleepy streets of San Antonio as though our lives depended on our arriving at a certain destination in a given length of time. I had no idea what the hurry was all about, but asked no questions.

My companion mumbled several times, "Student, ain't you, Kid?" People stared at us as we passed them, and no wonder. My companion walked in a peculiar manner, jerking and jumping as he stepped with frenzied feet.

He was in the middle thirties, a thin and wasted figure of a man, with yellow skin on his bones. His trousers were torn in zigzag fashion in many places, through which hairy skin showed. A large safety pin fastened his blue shirt over his breast. On one foot he had a button shoe, and on the other a shoe which laced. It was fastened with a white cord. His hair had once been black, but it was now streaked grey and straggled.

We came to a cheap drug store. "I know a guy here," he said, then tersely aside to me, "Wait."

I walked down to the next corner and waited. Presently he came toward me, the back of his right hand rubbing his left nostril. I noticed his face had a keener expression on it. He walked along with me as before, and still mumbled the same sentence, this time adding another word, "Hungry! Student, ain't you, Kid?" The youngster on the road is called a student by many of the older tramps. This is an appropriate name. For he attends a hard and ever changing school.

Feeling that the tramp had money, and that I might be saved the necessity of begging at back doors for food, I remained with him, and hopefully waited.

We passed one restaurant, and then another, but the man apparently did not see them. We stopped in an alley while he nervously twitched his muscles and contracted his right hand until the fingers were closed and the thumb stuck out rigid, forming a hole between it and the first finger. With incredible speed, he put a preparation in the hole and breathed it into his nostrils with frenzy, his eyes rolling as his head circled around.

Never having spoken more than a mumbled sentence at a time, he now began talking more fluently.

We passed another restaurant, but food was not considered by the man whose mind was rolling through infinite space. I stopped and said, "Listen, I'd like to get a feed." The man looked alarmed for a minute and hesitated. In desperation, I clutched his forearm. He yelled, "Ouch! Don't do that," and rubbed the arm beneath his sleeve. It was purple and festered and full of holes made by a hypodermic needle.

We entered the restaurant where I ordered food. The man looked on, mumbling, "My name's Peter. I am one o' the twelve. Student, ain't you, Kid?"

He rattled a dollar on the counter, and I picked up the change. The waiter busied himself with some tables in the rear, and I, well fed, was in the mood to talk.

I asked the man several questions, and received disjointed answers. Finally, I said, "Have you got any folks living?"

He answered tersely, "Nope, – wife dead, all dead, – hope dead."

Then suddenly, placing his head near me, he said, "Listen, shh! shh! I'll tell you somethin' if you don't tell no one. I'm St. Peter. I betrayed Him. I denied Him. I stay on the road so's He won't find me. When I hear roosters crowin' it makes me think of Him. I did Him a dirty trick, an' He was a good guy. They tell you I was the first Pope. That's the bunk. The first Pope was a Jew. He run a hock shop in Rome. Be quiet though. If they knew I told you, they'd ditch me off every train goin'."

He ran his claw-like hands through his grey streaked hair, and then pointed at the ceiling. "See them stars up there. I fixed them where they are. It was some job. I knew God when He was a kid. We went to school together. He was all right till He bought the world, – then He got the swell head. I worked with Him 'leven hundred years gittin' the sky fixed up. We raised the world up on big derricks. It sunk in one place and God got His foot caught under it. Hurt it bad. He swore like hell. We used two oceans of glue stickin' the stars in. We had an airplane longer'n a railroad. We shot the stars out of the airplane with a big cannon eighty-eight miles long. We sailed a thousand miles a minute, and God sure could whiz that ship around. Once His whiskers caught in the propeller. It darn near fixed us.

"We had a good time when we wasn't workin', though. We knew a lot of girl angels that come sailin' over to us on clouds. We lived in a peach of a house. Red lilies and purple grass an' everything around it.

"I got sore at God one time. I wanted to draw a million dollars to get a pint of booze with. He turned me down after I'd worked a whole day for it. So I quit Him cold and started to get even by buildin' a big bowl out of lumber right inside the sky. I wanted to shut out the light from His little old earth, just to show Him He couldn't bamboozle me that way. I sure got a bunch of lumber for the job. I started to shut out the sun and moon too.

"We sure had a time gettin' the sun up there. We kept it in cakes of ice bigger'n Texas, an' she'd sizzle 'em right up.

"I talked to God when I was half through, an' He said, 'All right, old boy, I'll let you go to it, but just remember, I'm God. I've built a lot of little old worlds like this one, and you can't slip nothing over on me. I can roll the mountains under you like little balls. I can make them shrivel like a kid's marble, and go whirlin' around like specks of dirt. I don't bother about plannin' things. I just get worlds started and turn people loose in them, hatched out of monkey eggs. Then I watch them for the fun of the thing. I've seen a million worlds go to hell in my time. They had generals and poets and statesmen that thought they were the whole works. I snapped my fingers – Bingo! – Zooey! – Where's the big men of fifty thousand years ago? Go to it, old kid. You won't get far.'

"I had Him worried though, for I kept pluggin' along, and was about all done. Everywhere you looked, you could see boards, and the sun peekin' through the cracks. She was gettin' darker down below, and I was sure workin' up high.

"The people kept shriekin' for light, but God couldn't give 'em none. I even saw Him laughin' at them.

"Finally, they sent big airships up after me, but I'd watch the men freeze, and the ships turn white with cold and go shootin' down like snowflakes. A lot of other airplanes followed till it looked like a snowstorm, and God comes bumpin' over to me on a green cloud trimmed in pink, and said, 'Good God! What the devil are you doin'?' You've got to figger it would take a thousand years to get up to me. Big eagles flew at me with wings longer'n a train, and beaks that twisted around, big as a ship. They was afraid of my hammer. Lots of men a hundred feet long flew around without heads too. And comets! Say! you never saw no fireworks like them. The stars whizzed aroun' like lightnin' bugs. One time two of them bumped into each other and sparks flew bigger'n houses on fire.

"When I had the sky about all nailed up, God was almost cryin'. His beard was blowin' in the breeze a mile long. Then He bumped into me on a cloud, and I rapped my thumb with the hammer and started to fall – and all the way down, for a hundred years, I saw little pieces of whitelike frozen airplanes sailin' all aroun' me."

An engine whistled. "Well, so long," yelled the man who worked with God, as he dashed out of the place, and ran like a madman toward the yards.

Chapter XXVII
A Woman Remembered

MISERY CRAWLS TO MISERY for the reason that it can crawl nowhere else.... That it gains solace thereby is rather an uneven possibility.

I lived much among the women of looser sex in my youth because I was able to obtain a certain amount of understanding from them, and as understanding is near to sympathy, the latter also.

Rabbit Town was that section of St. Marys where men only went at night. It consisted of some frame houses furnished with tawdry attempts at finery. Edna lived in one of these houses.

Edna was not quite eighteen. She had been seduced by her own father at fourteen and then an older brother carried on the work. She had a very low opinion of men.

Edna was beautiful. Her hair shone like yellow corn silk in the sun. Her eyes were a deep and vivid brown and they contrasted strangely with her yellow hair which she often wore unbraided down her back. She was slender, and moved with the grace of a fawn. She had a strong sex appeal, the only extenuating circumstance for the degenerate father and brother. When men enter the bawdy houses of the middle west, a bell is rung, and the girl inhabitants file in that the male may have his choice. Edna appealed so strongly to many men that the landlady, not wishing to work a faithful animal to death, as it were, would often keep her back, or, in many cases charge two dollars for her services instead of one.

Edna had shot her father and wounded her brother in a state bounding Ohio. Neither is Edna her first name, as I still like her, and would do no one thing to injure her getting along in a social system that is full of prudes and prudence.

Edna had never read a book that I know of, though I read paperbound copies of *Sappho* and *Camille* to her, and later, *From the Ballroom to Hell,* by some hell of a writer.

But Edna had a certain gift. It was the gift of wonder. She wondered about everything – about the sun and the moon and why the world was round, and how we happened to be here and who God's father was, and if he worked for a living. She was a sophisticated and charming young person, and was one of the few underworld women I ever met who was not a sentimentalist.

She kept me in affluence for some months, such as it was. She earned about one hundred and fifty dollars a week, but the landlady took half of that amount. Then Edna had other expenses, the heaviest among them being a thousand dollars which she owed to the lawyer who had secured her acquittal on the charge of murder. She sent twenty-five dollars to this man every week. Edna was soft spoken. Her voice was well modulated, and she never became angry. Her mother was dead, and Edna had kept house for the father and brother. She was naturally kindly and responded to kindness from the vilest sinner. She seemed to have taken the men's sex desire for fatherly and brotherly affection.

At fifteen she ran away to ——— in a delicate condition. She went to a hospital and told the head nurse of her condition, as she wanted to talk to a person of her own sex. That woman heard the story and said tersely, "I'd shoot 'em both if it was me!"

Edna replied, "I think I will!"

She worked in the hospital until it was time for her confinement. The baby came, opened its eyes two or three times, and went away again. Edna was nearly strangled with grief.

The great-hearted head nurse held the broken young mother in her arms and said, "Shoot them, God damn them!"

Edna left the hospital in five weeks. The head nurse loaned her twenty-five dollars, which she paid back. She bought a little blue revolver and returned to her father's house.

She walked alone, a worn and tired little blonde girl to the grave of her mother at the foot of the Blue Ridge Mountains.

Over that grave the child knelt while the sun turned the green of the mountains brown.

"Mother," she said, "I hope you can see me, I'm going to kill your man!" She sat there among the ragweeds and withered geraniums that covered the grave until the sun rolled behind the mountains. Her father would be home from work at six. It was time to go.

As everybody knew her in the town her walk homeward was somewhat retarded. "Gee, you've been away off to Cincinnati, hain't you, Edna!" "Yes," replied Edna, "I've been much farther than that!"

"My, it must be great to travel," said the woman all unknowing, as Edna walked on.

An ancient cat met her at the gate, and rubbed against her well-shaped ankles, remembering. She entered the house without knocking. Her father was preparing the evening meal. He leaned over the kitchen stove with a skillet in his hand. Her brother sat peeling potatoes on a stool nearby.

She looked about the kitchen. The father turned, in surprise at seeing her, and died the next moment. Two bullets ripped through his brain, and he fell across the hot stove and rolled on the floor.

The brother jumped and ran quickly through the door, a bullet flying after him and going through his left lung.

Edna walked quietly to the police station and said, "I've killed my father and brother with this gun. I told my mother I would this afternoon!"

She was six months in jail, and was tried and acquitted. She told me this tale one evening when the lights burned low in Rabbit Town.

It was on Sunday night, and Edna was weary from the night before. The landlady had allowed her to spend the afternoon and night in her room. So Edna was not at home to the leading business men of the town. She chose to spend her time smoking and drinking with a vagabond kid.

She often became melancholy over the little child who left the hospital so quickly. To relieve herself she would say, "Oh, well, dammit, it wouldn't have lived anyhow, besides, it was that dead bastard's – one of them." And then once, in a sweeping afterthought. "But Jimmy, it was mother's grandson, twice!"

Edna had been intimate with her lawyer, but not out of love for him. "He was kind to me, and that was all I had to give him," she said. "Besides," she continued, "after a girl once gets started it's hard to stop!"

"Would you go straight, Edna," I once asked her, "if you could?" "Sure," she answered, "but I've got to pay that damn lawyer, and I won't scrub any hussy's kitchen to do it. To hell with morals!"

"Would you be happier out of a sporting house?"

"Are you happier out of one?" she asked me in return.

"I wonder if my baby did die, you don't think they'd take it from me, do you, Jimmy?"

"No, I don't think so, the head nurse wouldn't do that."

"You can't tell what anybody'll do," Edna replied.

"The only thing that gets me is that men are such damn fools. They come down here and brag about their daughters and their half dead wives and get peeved because we don't love our heads off for them. I get so I never want to see a man again."

Edna was an inmate of the house when the landlady died.

The landlady was over six feet tall and raw-boned. She had a hard face that blended the buzzard and the eagle, but her heart was kind.

She had long suffered from palpitation of the heart and I once heard her say to Edna, "I'll kick off in a minute one of these days!" She did. She was dusting the picture of a naked woman on the housemaid's afternoon off. Her heart missed a beat or two, she gasped and fell, and hurried away to join Edna's baby.

The landlady had been everybody's friend and her loss was really felt. She had once told Edna to allow a struggling young undertaker to bury her if she died. "He's not a bad kid an' he may's well have the dough's anybody!"

The young undertaker came and laid her out in a purple coffin on cushions soft as down. Her old face had a weird smile upon it as if she were saying, "It's a hell of a mess, don't wake me up!"

There was much excitement in the town when the landlady went to seat herself on the right hand of God. Many beautiful flowers came. No names were signed to them. One might care for an ancient harlot in private, but it certainly is not proper to allow the public to know of it.

"Just think of it, Jimmy," said Edna, "I've slept with half the business men in this town, and there isn't a one of them with nerve enough to sign his name to a card. What a lot of crooked devils they are!"

But the landlady smiled sardonically through it all. A heavy gold wedding ring was on her third finger. The bauble of romance was going to the grave with her for the worms to crawl through.

Three moral ladies called at the house and suggested casually that it might be a good idea to bury the landlady at night. Edna became at once the girl who shot her father. Without raising her voice she said, "Mother goes out of this house in broad daylight and if they don't like it they can pull down their God damn blinds!"

"But," said one of the ladies, "we must think of the children of the town."

"The children of the town be damned. Don't make me laugh while Mother's lying dead."

The funeral was held at two that afternoon, and when the lid was clamped over the sardonically smiling old lady with the heavy wedding ring, Edna broke into a spasm of weeping.

No minister was invited and a bartender said a few words. "She never turned a down and out guy down and she always went fifty-fifty with everybody. She kept a bunch of guys in this town from goin' to the wall but they ain't here to own up to it now." The coffin was carried out of the house, and two white horses took it to the graveyard. Before the first shovelful of dirt was thrown in, a slight wind blew some yellow and green leaves into the grave. Then everyone turned away.

The sardonic mitigator of sex was at last completely alone.

No one came to the house after the funeral, so I spent the evening with Edna.

"You know, now that Mother's gone, I'm going to beat it out of here one of these days. It won't be long till I have that lawyer paid up and then I'm going so darn far it'll take a dollar to send me a postal card. I hate goodbyes and everything like that, they give me the blues, so if I slip out of here quick and you don't see me again, don't get sore, for that's the way I'm made!"

"That's all right," was my answer.

In two days she left the town without saying a word to anybody. A card came to me from Chicago, and then life closed around her.

I once sent a letter of enquiry to her lawyer. The word came back from his partner that he was dead and that Edna had not been heard of.

I hope greatly that she may read these lines.

Chapter XXVIII
Happenings

WHEN I TOOK TO THE ROAD AGAIN, the entire force of the Southern Pacific seemed in arms against me. I was ditched three times, travelling the short distance to El Rio. I eventually arrived there, and shared some crude food with a Mexican. That night I rode a banana special out "on the rods." It turned cold, and the wind whipped under the cars. The speeding train threw sand and stones upward, and they rattled against the bottom of the car like hail on a roof. I kept my eyes closed. Cords were tied about the bottoms of my trouser legs to keep the wind out. The wheels pounded over the steel rails in an endless rhythm, and the monotony of sound all but lulled me to sleep, in spite of the bumpy road, the flying train, and the volley of stones and sand.

I crawled from underneath with aching muscles when the train stopped at R———.

It was too early for breakfast, as the smoke was just rising from the cottages of the poor. I remember looking at the unpainted houses, the withered lawns, and the ugly streets, and feeling glad that I was a hobo on a long free trail.

The rising sun made the rude houses stand out in ugly outline. But as I was not in search of beauty, but of breakfast, I soon started "battering the back doors."

There was a systematic unkindness about seven housewives in one dingy block. They treated me with no more courtesy than if I had been a book agent, or a minister begging funds for a new Church. One irate woman slammed the door in my face, and as I hurried away, a dog nipped the calf of my leg. The woman opened the door again and laughed. It was the hard laugh of a heartless woman. It echoed down the smudgy street, and could be heard above the barking of the class-conscious dog. Picking up a piece of brick sharper than the mongrel's teeth, I flung it viciously through the air, as only the son of a race of brick-throwing Irish could throw it. It hummed a red tune as it went. The woman, now silent, stood in the yard and watched the trained tramp-hater retreat in her direction. She yelled loudly at him. The brick hit him right under the tail. That end of the animal hunched down. The other end let out an unearthly yell, that reverberated through the quiet street. The woman shook her fist at me as I blazed part of a brick at her. The brick crashed against the side of the house. The dog, still yelping, hurried around the house, and left me the defiant and hungry master of the situation.

I finally got a "set down" several blocks away. Another woman made up for the harsh treatment accorded me, and my sensitive spirit was appeased. Her daughter stood near with the kindest dancing eyes. She was not any older than myself. Her hair, tied with a red ribbon, hung in a long black braid. Her percale dress outlined her lovely form. Her mother did me the honour to sit at table with me.

I expanded under such treatment and told a lurid tale, which ended when a knock was heard at the front door. The girl answered it. A man's rough voice asked, "Seen anything of a tramp this way? He like to cave in Mrs. Muldowney's house an' dog with a brick. He ran this way."

There was a pause for a brief moment, and my heart pounded fast. Then the answer came clear and distinct, "No – we haven't seen him. We are afraid of tramps, and we never answer the door if we think one is near." I heard the man grunt and the door close. I was flabbergasted when the girl returned to the kitchen. What could words of mine say to thank her? Unstrung from the hard riding of the night before, I choked back a sob.

I tried to thank her.

"You mustn't think of that," she answered with a dimpled smile. "Brother was away on freights for two whole months. He told us all about it. He's in the Navy now."

"I don't understand why boys knock about so," said the mother as she watched the officer walking down the street.

Years later, when haunted by the ghosts of road memories, I have often thought of the woman and the red-ribboned girl with the dancing eyes of wonder. I can see them as I write, though seventeen years have staggered by like wounded drunkards in the rain.

I left the good woman's home and walked toward the centre of the town, carrying a "handout" which solved my eating problem for the day. As I reached the court-house square, a crowd yelled madly. They stood in front of the court-house jail yelling loudly at someone inside. Some broken iron bars hung from a third story window. Soon the end of a rope was thrown from the window to the waiting crowd below. Many men grabbed it. Framed in the window, with a rope around his neck, and men screaming behind him, was a negro, with eyes as big as eggs.

"Kill the nigger! Kill the nigger!" yelled many voices. "Pop his neck. Make it crack."

The negro's face writhed in fear, as women, men and children hurried from all directions into the square.

A terrific shout went up, and the rope was jerked by many men. The black body shot into space, whirled, and fell crashing into a tree. "Don't shoot," screamed a voice.

A man untangled the wriggling body, and, shaking and horror-stricken, it fell to the ground. They dragged the half-conscious negro to the business square, where a fire burned slowly.

He was placed upright above it, his armpits in heavy post-like crutches.

As the shoes were ripped off, the blaze burned his feet. He wriggled his body frantically as more fuel was placed on the fire and the flame shot upward. "Not too fast," yelled a voice. "Let him burn slow." The doomed Ethiopian's eyes rolled swiftly as the poles were knocked from under and his body fell into the fire. A blood-curdling "Ouch, ouch, O God! Oh, ouch, O God, O God hab mercy."

"We'll mercy you – you black bastard," yelled a man.

The poles were made upright, and the negro's armpits were fitted into the crutch-like end of them. Wriggling loose, the black mortal tried to eat fire to end his agony. That boon was denied him. A club crashed his wrist. His head went on his breast. His eyes closed a moment, and as the blaze shot higher, they opened in awful pain.

The clothes burned first, and then the flame ate the hair from his skull. The ears charred and melted on his head. He moaned in prolonged and dying pain, "ooooo-ooch, oo-oh-oh-oh."

The burnt body fell from its moorings, and the poles dropped over it. Kerosene was thrown on the hissing fire.

Sick at heart, I turned away. Some children skipped the death-rope gracefully.

Chapter XXIX
A Train Passes

THE NOVEMBER RAINS poured steadily down and bathed all Texas in bedraggled wretchedness. At times, the slowly falling rain seemed to pause mid-air, as if weary of the monotony of falling downward.

El Paso was the next division point – and it was a day's ride away. The distance across Texas is one-fourth of the distance across America, or more. It stretches a thousand miles.

I succeeded in riding a freight train about two miles out of one division. It was stopped and searched vigorously. I was discovered clinging like a wet rat to the rods underneath. Two other hoboes were also ditched.

A young brakeman explained tersely, but not unkindly, that the conductor had been given a three-months' lay-off because tramps had ridden his trains in great numbers. The train went on without us. A fire burned in the woods some distance away. A roof was built to keep the rain out. A hole was cut through the top to allow the smoke to escape. An open place in the woods afforded a view of the tracks.

Hoboes crowded near the fire. Their steaming clothes hung wrinkled on their bodies. Some elbowed their way to the welcome blaze as politely as respectable citizens crowding on a street car. Others held back that some more wet and wretched vagabond might be given a place near the fare.

There was one sickly looking tramp, with weak face, yellow as gold and shrivelled like parchment long dried in the sun. A brutal-appearing tramp pushed the half-dead vagabond in front of him, while others gave way. The wasted wretch muttered an ineffectual thanks and rubbed his clammy hands together.

In one corner of the place, a "mulligan" was cooking in an immense pot. A mulligan is a combination of nearly everything cookable. It is the common fare of hoboland.

When the food was ready, we gathered ravenously about it. There were not enough tin cups, or plates of any kind to hold it. The "jungle" had recently been raided by the citizens.

We looked under the dripping trees for rusty dishes that had been scattered about.

An engine whistle was heard. It startled the vagabonds. Surprise, chagrin, dismay registered in turn on their faces. "Damn the luck," a tramp said, "but I stay here'n eat."

None of us moved in the direction of the train, which rolled slowly westward. "If you were on that baby, you'd be in El Paso in the mornin'," grinned a hobo with a hangman's expression.

"Oh, well, somethin' else'll pull out before sundown," added a tramp consolingly.

"Afore sundown, hell! The sun ain't been up for a week," snarled another.

When the stew was eaten, we held the dishes in the rain to be cleaned by nature. The day wore on, and not a living thing moved. Birds huddled in the trees. It became dark by the middle of the afternoon. Clouds of misty fog settled everywhere.

A half dozen hoboes went for water in the direction of the railroad. They could not be seen a hundred yards from the fire.

There were only potatoes left, and it was the intention to make soup. They were peeled with pocket knives, called "frogstickers."

When the men returned with water, the potatoes were thrown into the vessel and it was splashed on top of them. Some wet salt from a rusty can was added.

While the soup cooked, we returned to the business of keeping up the fire, the hardest job being to find wood that was dry enough to burn.

When the soup was ready, we crowded about it. A whistle blew. A light pierced through the fog. A train was creeping west. We made for the rods, which would keep us out of the rain.

"Let them jungle buzzards have that junk. It's no good anyhow," said the man with the hangman's expression.

As I started to crawl underneath a car, I heard a loud clicking, as of loose iron striking the rails underneath. For fear of the danger involved, I clambered between two cars and stood on the bumpers. On many "hostile" divisions a long wire is fastened to the cars, at the end of which is an iron coupling which lies on the ground between the cars. As the train speeds along, the iron weight is thrown upward under the cars, dealing out death to the tramp whom it strikes.

The train ran a short distance and stopped at a water tank, near which were a few scattered houses.

I left the train, feeling that anything was better than the misery of the ride through the rain. Other men joined me, among them the man with the face like a hangman.

"That rattler's got irons under her. I near got nipped twice. No wonder they didn't try to ditch us – thought we'd git killed anyhow," he said.

The only shelter available at first was the water tank. It stood high above the track on wooden beams, down which the water ran.

The train melted into the rainy night. Then all that could be heard was the far-off whistle of the engine and the maddening patter of rain. Our spirits were as low as the ground. To cheer our water-soaked hearts, we talked of California, still a thousand miles away.

Many wet hours dripped by before another train crawled over the rails.

When it finally came, we boarded a coal car loaded with railroad ties, as all the other cars were sealed. We were not molested, as the train men did not look for hoboes on such a night.

CHAPTER XXX
STEEL TRAIL'S END

WE QUICKLY BUILT A WALL of ties in a corner of the car, and then placed other ties above for a roof. One of the men extracted newspapers from an inner pocket. We fastened them on the rude ceiling and walls to keep the rain from seeping through the cracks. We then placed ties in front and crawled through an opening which we left near the top where the wall nearly joined the ceiling.

The noise of the bumping train did not entirely diminish the rattling of wind and rain outside.

All the derelicts smoked, while I huddled in a corner and watched the matches glow against their road-marked faces. The brutal-looking befriender of the yellow man smoked a pipe, the stem of which curved downward over his square chin. The bowl of the pipe was large, and the burning tobacco glowed within.

Wet gypsies of life we were, asking little, and getting less, and deserving less than that.

I left the rovers in El Paso, determined to make more progress in the remaining eight hundred miles of the journey to Los Angeles.

After begging a late breakfast, and a "hand-out" in the Mexican quarters, I again returned to the yards.

The railroad detectives were particularly vigilant at this time, as tramps had left the hatchways of banana cars open, and five carloads had frozen.

The trains were watched closely, and many vagabonds were arrested and taken to the city jail. I watched four of them being led away by two railraod bulls. Among them was the man who looked like a hangman. He saw me peeking at him from around the box car, but he gave no sign of recognition, for fear, no doubt, that it would direct the attention of his captors toward me.

I hurried westward until the web of tracks merged into two single strands. These I followed for several miles in the hope of finding a grade that would compel the trains to run more slowly.

It had turned much colder, and great snowflakes fell. A flurry of wind came and the atmosphere cleared slightly in the west for a brief space of time. Outlined in the distance was the high, uneven ridge of a mountain that crawled darkly like a long reptile above a grey mass of snow-dripping clouds.

The mountain outline faded away, the air became still, and the day became darker. Even larger flakes of snow fell.

I was miserable and wretchedly cold. My shoes were soaked, and my numbed feet struck the ground heavily.

Arriving at an elevation, I waited for hours in the white wet weather. Not a soul drew near, and not a sound was heard. I ate the "handout," feeling all the while that I would gladly trade all the food in the world for a warm stimulant. I became obsessed with a desire for warm coffee.

Suddenly, far off, a strong light made the falling snow glisten in the air. A whistle rumbled low and long.

My heart beat with nervous tension, as the train thundered on toward me.

The great engine approached in a blinding flash of light. I circled about a telegraph post until it passed. The head brakeman, and another man, possibly a dick, stood in the cab of the engine.

Several cars passed me, and I started forward, while scanning the ground for an even spot on which to run with the swiftly running train.

I was determined to hang on even if my arms were jerked loose. With that resolve, I picked out a car and ran with it. My hands clutched the iron ladder, and held fast. My neck creaked, and my muscles ached.

When I recovered my faculties, I climbed to the top of the wet car and crawled to the centre of it. I stretched, head downward, on the slanting roof and felt the edge of the door. It was open about six inches. I knew from the general make-up of the train, its great engine, and the red tags tacked to the cars, that it was a fast freight, second only in running time to a mail train.

I wondered what could be in the car, a carload of coke for which a factory waited, perhaps. It was the only kind of a car that would have open doors. Hoboes would not steal coke, and besides, its gaseous quality might cause spontaneous combustion if it were tightly sealed.

The train came to a grade. The puffing engine covered the train with a cloud of black smoke. I leaned halfway over the car, and braced my feet against the board walk on the roof, and heaved at the door with all my strength. It opened about a foot. I then turned about and slid down, feet foremost, clinging desperately all the while to the smooth wet boards. One slip, and I would roll on the ground. The door swayed a trifle while I held on and leaned far out. At last my feet touched something hard inside the car. Working my way inside, I found the car was loaded with large pieces of coke.

The jagged pieces of coke scratched my hands and tore my wet clothing. With only room enough to crawl, I made my way slowly to the end of the car.

There was a high embankment of coke at the end. I crawled over this, and there, sitting in the corner, was a little hobo with a ferret face. He was smoking.

"Hello, Kid, you made 'er, huh? She's some rambler."

The light from the door streamed weakly over him.

"I'll say she's a rambler," I replied breathlessly.

"Yep, I spotted 'er in the yards. This car's red tagged for Los Angels. I sneaked in an' fixed the coke this way. Them bulls hate to crawl over coke. If any of 'em comes to the door an yells, 'Hey, come on out or I'll shoot,' sh ... jist lay still. They can't shoot through coke. That's a stall they have."

The tramp kept chattering, while I, weary and worried, stretched my coat on the coke, and adjusted the pieces so the jagged ends were as comfortable as possible. I then slept soundly.

The train stood still, and I rubbed my eyes. The little hobo near me was smoking.

"Where are we, 'Bo?" I asked.

"I don't know. It oughta be Maricopa. You been poundin' your ear since yisterday. You must be all in."

"You think you kin stand it to Los?" the tramp asked.

"I can if I don't starve," was my reply.

For hour after hour we rode through the desert into the green heart of California.

CHAPTER XXXI
WORDS

THERE FOLLOWED SEVERAL YEARS of wanderlust of which I eventually was cured. I lived in many a brothel where the dregs of life found shelter. I fraternized with human wrecks whose hands shook as if with palsy, with weaklings who cringed and whined at life, with degenerates and perverts, greasy and lousy, with dope fiends who would shoot needles of water into their arms to relieve the wild aching for an earthly Heaven. I learned the secrets of traitors and crawlers and other fakers.

Some of them were not even ambitious enough to beg, but would whimper at those who did. Fortunately for me, there had always been some chemical in my nature that had kept my mind active so that I was not allowed to rot in hives of congested humanity.

Tramping in wild and windy places, without money, food, or shelter, was better for me than supinely bowing to any conventional decree of fate.

The road gave me one jewel beyond price, the leisure to read and dream. If it made me old and wearily wise at twenty, it gave me for companions the great minds of all the ages, who talked to me with royal words.

When whipt of life and snubbed of prudes I could talk to old Sam Johnson with his strange blending of the naïve and the philosopher. I could still love Goldsmith. I could hear Chatterton saying – "I'm a poet, sir." I walked with him through the streets of London, I cried when he took the poison. I could stroll down an English lane with Coleridge and meet John Keats. I could stop while Keats turned and said, "Let me carry away the memory, Coleridge, of having held your hand." And I could hear Coleridge say afterward, "There's death in that hand."

I stole books from libraries. I stole them whenever I could. I would often carry two or three of them with me and hide them. It would not be wise for a bum to be caught with a library book. He would have to explain. Bums have so much to explain. It would be rather embarrassing.

I stole *The Story of an African Farm* from the library of the Newsboys' Home in Pittsburgh. I kept the book with me on the road for two weeks, tramping by slow stages to Chicago while reading it. The three children on that South African farm, Waldo, Lyndall and Emily, will remain with me, precious memories until the day I die. I once stole Dostoievsky's *Crime and Punishment* in a Colorado city. It was in two volumes, a fact I did not know at the time of the theft. Upon the discovery I was terribly mortified, and was forced to go back for the other volume. This incident exasperated me so much that I was very careful to steal complete volumes in the future.

Becoming dazed with the magnificent psychology of the epileptic Russian, I did not care whether I travelled or not, but stayed about the city and slept in a box car until I had finished that appalling book.

I was so grateful for the discovery of the book that I returned to the library and carried Dostoievsky's *House of the Dead* away with me. I carried the book with me for days. It was with me when I decided to work a few days as a dishwasher at a camp near Leadville.

To my horror one morning I discovered a mucker tearing a page from the book to use as shaving paper. I threw a cup at him, and battled him about the camp. No one could use a book of mine in such a manner.

I stole Boswell's *Johnson* and Gorky's *Creatures That Once Were Men* from an Alabama library. The Gorky book was shelf worn though the pages had never been cut. I still have the Boswell book and if the library will communicate with me and enclose postage I will be glad to return it to them.

I became very much interested in Chambers *Encyclopedia of English Literature* during an Indiana journey. It was in five large volumes. I thought it was no use for such books to remain in Indiana as there was a possibility of their never being read. For many days I considered the matter. I finally compromised with what was left of my conscience by deciding not to take them. They were so terribly large anyhow, and I had read a great deal of their contents while debating the best way of stealing them.

I once stole a beautifully bound small leather Bible from a preacher's house in New Haven, Connecticut. He had called me into his library after I had dined. The good man wore a 'come to Jesus' collar, a shoe string black tie and a Uriah Heep expression. But he was a very decent fellow for all of that. He talked long and earnestly to me and explained in detail that the wages of sin were death and that all the ways of the flesh were but hollow sounds and tinkling cymbals, that God took care of the weary and the worn. He asked me my parentage and I told him that my father had studied for the Methodist ministry but had died early of brain fever. His heart was touched, and I saw the great look of pity in his face and touched him for a silver dollar.

The Bible was lying on the living room centre table among many other books. The good man excused himself for a moment and I appropriated it.

Upon the minister's return we talked a little more about the wages of sin, and I took my departure, promising to be a better boy and write to him of my success.

Stealing that Bible was the luckiest thing I ever did. I journeyed on to Boston where all the policemen are religious, and was arrested for vagrancy. The policeman searched me and discovered the Bible. Right away he became interested, and I had to think fast. The blue coat talked with an Irish brogue. I told him that my uncle had been a priest in Ohio and had only been dead two months and that his death had given me the blues and I had gone on the road.

"Ay – what did he die of?" was the cop's question.

I told him that he had contracted typhoid fever and leprosy while nursing a man whom everyone had been afraid to go near.

"The holy man," said the policeman.

"Yes, he was holy – there was no one like him," I ventured.

The policeman lead me to the street curbing.

"You're a Catholic, ain't you, Kid?"

Hoping to God I was guessing right I replied, "You bet your life, I wouldn't be nothin' else, none o' them other religions are any good."

I hesitated for a second, hoping against hope that my capturer was not from the north of Ireland. He pulled his red and brown moustache and deliberated.

"Fine talk me lad," he said, "Come wit' me, I'll take you to the missus." He led me to a small brown house about two blocks away.

His wife was large and happy, and with a zest for life. She had a picture of Pope Leo XIII over the mantelpiece.

Her husband told my story for me while the good woman listened tearfully.

"Ay an' he carries a Bible wit' him does he … the poor, dear blessed childer. How glad I am ye found him Dan instead o' some o' thim Protestant booms on the force. Indade they'd make quick work of a lad like him.

"So your poor uncle died nursin' a sick man Sonny. Glory be to him. He's in Heaven now watchin' over you and how glad he is you still rade his Bible."

I touched the book quickly in my pocket as an alarming thought came to me…. It was a Protestant Bible…. Right away the answer came … my uncle wanted me to read both the Protestant and Catholic Bibles so I could discover for myself how beautiful the latter was…. But the question never came up. A Bible was a Bible in their opinion, and it never occurred to them to question me.

The policeman returned to his duty of protecting Boston from the Cabots and the Lodges while I remained and told lie after lie to his all trusting wife.

After talking for some time I left with a gift of money and a promise to write to her regularly.

That night I laughed over the incident with a fellow rover whom I met in a joint on Tremont Street.

The imaginative young vagabond quickly loses the social instincts that help to make life bearable for other men. Always he hears voices calling in the night from far-away places where blue waters lap strange shores. He hears birds singing and crickets chirping a luring roundelay. He sees the moon, yellow ghost of a dead planet, haunting the earth.

Travelling a brutal road, his moral code becomes heavy, and he often throws it away. Civilization never quite restores all of it to him, which, of course, may not be as tragic as it sounds.

Gorky, the brilliant ex-tramp, returned to the road again, for a year. Few people understood the reason. I did.

It was the caged eagle returning to the mountains of its youth for a last look at the carefree life it had known. It remained a year, and found that the vast and lonely places were the same, but the blood had slowed around the eagle heart, and it flew back to the valley again, wearier than before – the last illusion gone.

There are those who have solutions for all the ills of humanity. There are people who love the mob in the abstract, but keep away from the scum of life themselves.

I have never known a great idealist who had a profound knowledge of life. There is a blessed something that blurs their eyes when they look at the viciousness of it all. They turn away from it and blubber platitudes, like blind men in a forest listening to birds and hearing not the reptiles underneath.

They cannot see life around them, their eyes being fastened on the great dream ahead, a few million years after they are rotten. Some idealists are selfish as individuals, but lovers of the mob. And who can really love a mob?

Evolution helps the mob. One can only help the individual.

And wise men learn to expect gratitude in Heaven. It is too delicate a flower for the winds of this earth.

All hoboes know these things. Petty men themselves, they expect pettiness from others, and find it, as they deserve. The vast crowd of them are liars, ingrates, and thieves. They prey on the false sentiments of women like popular novelists. They chortle sad tales to the unsophisticated brooders of pauper children.

A famous writer of tramp life said that the poor always give to the poor. Writers should not make definite rules about humanity. They are always wrong.

Some of the poor give to hoboes, others do not. If I were to choose a sure means of eating, my past experience as a young vagabond would incline me toward the women of the underworld. I have begged every poverty-stricken house in a block, and have had sore knuckles for my pains. Again, I have begged in other poverty-stricken blocks, and have been well rewarded with food. Some races seem more kindly than others toward the beggar, but that, too, is a mooted question among the tramps themselves, though the German women are favored.

A clever young tramp, if he has that indefinable something called personality, can always beg money on the street with success. He must have a knowledge of human nature, however, and be able to distinguish one class of citizens from another. In the argot of the road a "good" bum is one who is always successful as a beggar. All in all, though, the most resourceful and energetic tramp gets the most food and money. It is possible that these qualities discount personality, as few tramps have anything pertaining to the latter after they are twenty years old. The road writes with heavy hand its lines of degeneracy, brutality, and all-around wretchedness on their faces and bodies.

All of the philosophical stuff written about tramps should be taken lightly. The non-producers of the nation are tramps in one sense or another. The prattling parasitic club woman, the obese gambler in bonds, the minister in a fashionable church, all are tramps who happen to have beds and bath, and the economic security that men go mad to obtain.

In fact, the tramp is merely a parasite who has not been admitted to society.

Many of the younger tramps can fight with fury. A hobo camp is not a Y.M.C.A. when trouble starts. Some great pugilists have been developed on the road. Jack Dempsey, Kid McCoy, and Stanley Ketchell, three of the greatest bruisers that ever lived, were youthful hoboes for several years.

Neither am I interested in sociology among tramps. All the writers of such drivel have not contributed one iota to the solution of the problem. There would be fewer men in penitentiaries if we could drive greed from our social system. A vast army of the men in hoboland and jails are recruited from orphanages and reform schools.

Perhaps a few more Judge Lindseys with understanding hearts would help a great deal. A thousand Judge Lindseys in America – but one may as well ask for a thousand Christs. Perhaps we need fewer mothers who know nothing of motherhood, and more women like Jane Addams.

My own opinion is that the greatest man of any era has made no dint at all in the armor-plate of his time. Some one may say that Christ did. Analyze the churches with an open mind, and the ravages of pseudo-Christianity.

But then, I am no reformer, but a weary writer who has been living in the memory of adventure.

My pity of life's wastrels is akin to love – my contempt is akin to hate – for they are, each and all, the beaten accidents of childhood. So always in kindlier moods, I agree with Masefield, sad vagabond of genius,

> "Others may sing of the wine and the wealth and the mirth,
> The portly presence of potentates goodly in girth; –
> Mine be the dirt and the dross, *the dust and the scum of the earth!*
> Theirs be the music, the color, the glory, the gold:
> Mine be a handful of ashes, a mouthful of mould,
> Of the maimed, of the halt and the blind in the rain and the cold –
> Of these shall my songs be fashioned, my tales be told. AMEN."

THE END

Other Titles from AK Press

Books

MARTHA **ACKELSBERG**—*Free Women of Spain*

KATHY **ACKER**—*Pussycat Fever*

MICHAEL **ALBERT**—*Moving Forward: Program for a Participatory Economy*

JOEL **ANDREAS**—*Addicted to War: Why the U.S. Can't Kick Militarism*

ALEXANDER **BERKMAN**—*What is Anarchism?*

HAKIM **BEY**—*Immediatism*

JANET **BIEHL** & PETER **STAUDENMAIER**—*Ecofascism: Lessons From The German Experience*

BIOTIC BAKING BRIGADE—*Pie Any Means Necessary: The Biotic Baking Brigade Cookbook*

JACK **BLACK**—*You Can't Win*

MURRAY **BOOKCHIN**—*Anarchism, Marxism, and the Future of the Left*

MURRAY **BOOKCHIN**—*Social Anarchism or Lifestyle Anarchism: An Unbridgeable Chasm*

MURRAY **BOOKCHIN**—*Spanish Anarchists: The Heroic Years 1868–1936, The*

MURRAY **BOOKCHIN**—*To Remember Spain: The Anarchist and Syndicalist Revolution of 1936*

MURRAY **BOOKCHIN**—*Which Way for the Ecology Movement?*

DANNY **BURNS**—*Poll Tax Rebellion*

CHRIS **CARLSSON**—*Critical Mass: Bicycling's Defiant Celebration*

JAMES **CARR**–*Bad*

NOAM **CHOMSKY**—*At War With Asia*

NOAM **CHOMSKY**—*Language and Politics*

NOAM **CHOMSKY**—*Radical Priorities*

WARD **CHURCHILL**—*On the Justice of Roosting Chickens: Reflections on the Consequences of U.S. Imperial Arrogance and Criminality*

HARRY **CLEAVER**—*Reading Capital Politically*

ALEXANDER **COCKBURN** & JEFFREY **ST. CLAIR** (ed.)—*Politics of Anti-Semitism, The*

ALEXANDER **COCKBURN** & JEFFREY **ST. CLAIR** (ed.)—*Serpents in the Garden*

DANIEL & GABRIEL **COHN-BENDIT**—*Obsolete Communism: The Left-Wing Alternative*

EG SMITH COLLECTIVE—*Animal Ingredients A–Z (3rd edition)*

VOLTAIRINE **de CLEYRE**—*Voltarine de Cleyre Reader*

HOWARD **EHRLICH**—*Reinventing Anarchy, Again*

SIMON **FORD**—*Realization and Suppression of the Situationist International: An Annotated Bibliography 1972–1992, The*

YVES **FREMION** & **VOLNY**—*Orgasms of History: 3000 Years of Spontaneous Revolt*

DANIEL **GUERIN**—*No Gods No Masters*

AGUSTIN **GUILLAMON**—*Friends Of Durruti Group, 1937–1939, The*

ANN **HANSEN**—*Direct Action: Memoirs Of An Urban Guerilla*

WILLIAM **HERRICK**—*Jumping the Line: The Adventures and Misadventures of an American Radical*

FRED **HO**—*Legacy to Liberation: Politics & Culture of Revolutionary Asian/Pacific America*

STEWART **HOME**—*Assault on Culture*

STEWART **HOME**—*Neoism, Plagiarism & Praxis*

STEWART **HOME**—*Neoist Manifestos / The Art Strike Papers*

STEWART **HOME**—*No Pity*

STEWART **HOME**—*Red London*

STEWART **HOME**—*What Is Situationism? A Reader*

JAMES **KELMAN**—*Some Recent Attacks: Essays Cultural And Political*

KEN **KNABB**—*Complete Cinematic Works of Guy Debord*

KATYA **KOMISARUK**—*Beat the Heat: How to Handle Encounters With Law Enforcement*

NESTOR **MAKHNO**—*Struggle Against The State & Other Essays, The*

G.A. **MATIASZ**—*End Time*

CHERIE **MATRIX**—*Tales From the Clit*

ALBERT **MELTZER**—*Anarchism: Arguments For & Against*

ALBERT **MELTZER**—*I Couldn't Paint Golden Angels*

RAY **MURPHY**—*Siege Of Gresham*

NORMAN **NAWROCKI**—*Rebel Moon*

HENRY **NORMAL**—*Map of Heaven, A*

HENRY **NORMAL**—*Dream Ticket*

HENRY **NORMAL**—*Fifteenth of February*

HENRY **NORMAL**—*Third Person*

FIONBARRA **O'DOCHARTAIGH**—*Ulster's White Negroes: From Civil Rights To Insurrection*

DAN **O'MAHONY**—*Four Letter World*

CRAIG **O'HARA**—*Philosophy Of Punk, The*

ANTON **PANNEKOEK**—*Workers' Councils*

BEN **REITMAN**—*Sister of the Road: the Autobiography of Boxcar Bertha*

PENNY **RIMBAUD**—*Diamond Signature, The*

PENNY **RIMBAUD**—*Shibboleth: My Revolting Life*

RUDOLF **ROCKER**—*Anarcho-Syndicalism*

RON **SAKOLSKY** & STEPHEN **DUNIFER**—*Seizing the Airwaves: A Free Radio Handbook*

ROY **SAN FILIPPO**—*New World In Our Hearts: 8 Years of Writings from the Love and Rage Revolutionary Anarchist Federation, A*

CDs

DVDs

ORDERING INFORMATION

AK Press
674-A 23rd Street,
Oakland, CA 94612-1163,
USA

Phone: (510) 208-1700
E-mail: akpress@akpress.org
URL: www.akpress.org
Please send all payments (checks, money orders, or cash at your own risk) in
U.S. dollars. Alternatively, we take VISA and MC.

AK Press
PO Box 12766,
Edinburgh, EH8 9YE,
Scotland

Phone: (0131) 555-5165
E-mail: ak@akedin.demon.uk
URL: www.akuk.com
Please send all payments (cheques, money orders, or cash at your own risk)
in U.K. pounds. Alternatively, we take credit cards.

For a dollar, a pound or a few IRC's, the same addresses would be delighted
to provide you with the latest complete AK catalog, featuring several
thousand books, pamphlets, zines, audio products and stylish apparel published & distributed by AK Press. Alternatively, check out our websites for
the complete catalog, latest news and updates, events, and secure ordering.

www.ingramcontent.com/pod-product-compliance
Lightning Source LLC
Jackson TN
JSHW020019141224
75386JS00025B/607